SLAVERY IN AMERICAN HISTORY

VOICES FROM SLAVERY'S PAST

YEARNING TO BE HEARD

SUZANNE CLOUD TAPPER

FOREWORD BY SERIES ADVISOR
DR. HENRY LOUIS GATES, JR.

Enslow Publishers, Inc.

40 Industrial Road   PO Box 38
Box 398   Aldershot
Berkeley Heights, NJ 07922   Hants GU12 6BP
USA   UK

http://www.enslow.com

Library of Congress Cataloging-in-Publication Data

Cloud Tapper, Suzanne.
    Voices from slavery's past: yearning to be heard / Suzanne Cloud Tapper.
        p. cm. — (Slavery in American history)
    Includes bibliographical references and index.
    ISBN 0-7660-2157-2
    1. Slaves—United States—Biography—Juvenile literature. 2. African Americans—
Biography—Juvenile literature. 3. Slavery—United States—History—Juvenile
literature. 4. Slaveholders—United States—Biography—Juvenile literature.
[1. Slaves. 2. African Americans—Biography. 3. Slavery—History. 4. Slaveholders.]
I. Title. II. Series.
E444.C64 2004
973'.0496073-dc22

                                                    2003025134

Printed in the United States of America

10 9 8 7 6 5 4 3 2 1

To Our Readers: We have done our best to make sure all Internet Addresses in this
book were active and appropriate when we went to press. However, the author and
the publisher have no control over and assume no liability for the material available
on those Internet sites or on other Web sites they may link to. Any comments or
suggestions can be sent by e-mail to comments@enslow.com or to the address on the
back cover.

Illustration Credits: Bridgeman Photos, p. 104; © Corbis, pp. 3, 105; Enslow
Publishers, Inc., pp. 1 (bottom left), 25, 59, 63, 64, 96; Every Effort has been made to
locate all copyright holders of these photos: pp. 1 (bottom, second from left), 69;
Hemera Technologies, Inc, p. 55; Hulton Archive/Getty Images, pp. 1 (top, second from
left), 22; © Jane Reed, Harvard News Office, p. 5; Courtesy Library of Congress, Brady-
Handy Collection, Reproduced from the *Dictionary of American Portraits*, published by
Dover Publications, Inc., in 1967, pp. 1 (bottom right), 89; National Archives and
Records Administration, p. 109; North Wind Picture Archives, pp. 11, 17, 61, 80;
Reproduced from the Collections of the Library of Congress, pp. 1 (top and bottom,
second from right), 6–7, 26, 33, 40, 53, 73, 74, 76, 87, 92; Reproduced from the
Dictionary of American Portraits, published by Dover Publications, Inc., in 1967, pp. 1
(top right), 45, 50; Superstock, p. 35; T/Maker Company/Brøderbund Software, Inc.,
p. 38; University of Virginia Library, pp.1 (top left), 8.

Cover Illustration: © Corbis (Frederick Douglass speaking); Enslow Publishers, Inc.,
(Background Map).

✈ C O N T E N T S ✦

FOREWORD BY SERIES ADVISOR
HENRY LOUIS GATES, JR.   4

1 HENRY BIBB: ESCAPE
   TO FREEDOM   7

2 JOHN NEWTON:
   SLAVE MERCHANT   21

3 OLAUDAH EQUIANO:
   GOODBYE TO AFRICA   31

4 JOSEPH LE CONTE:
   SCIENCE AND RACISM.   44

5 LETITIA BURWELL:
   PAMPERED BLINDNESS.   57

6 HARRIET JACOBS:
   DESPERATE TO LIVE FREE   68

7 DOUGLASS AND GARRISON:
   DOWN WITH SLAVERY.   83

8 LEGACY OF HATE   99

   TIMELINE   111

   CHAPTER NOTES   113

   GLOSSARY.   123

   FURTHER READING.   124

   INTERNET ADDRESSES AND
   HISTORIC SITES.   125

   INDEX   126

American Slavery's Undying Legacy

While the Thirteenth Amendment outlawed slavery in the United States in 1865, the impact of that institution continued to be felt long afterward, and in many ways is still being felt today. The broad variety of experiences encompassed within that epoch of American history can be difficult to encapsulate. Enslaved, free, owner, trader, abolitionist: each "category" hides a complexity of experience as varied as the number of individuals who occupied these identities.

One thing is certain: in spite of how slavery has sometimes been portrayed, very few, if any, enslaved blacks were utter victims who quietly and passively accepted such circumstances. Those who claimed ownership over Africans and African Americans used violence, intimidation, and other means to wield a great degree of power and control. But as human beings—and as laborers within an economic system that depended on labor—all enslaved blacks retained varying degrees of agency within that system.

The "Slavery in American History" series provides a strong and needed overview of the most important aspects of American slavery, from the first transport of African slaves to the American colonies, to the long fight for abolition, to the lasting impact of slavery on America's economy, politics, and culture. Only by understanding American slavery and its complex legacies can we begin to understand the challenge facing not just African Americans, but all Americans: To make certain that our country is a living and breathing embodiment of the principles enunciated in the Constitution of the United States. Only by understanding the past can we mend the present and ensure the rights of our future generations.

—**Henry Louis Gates, Jr.,** *Ph.D., W.E.B. Du Bois Professor of the Humanities, Chair of the Department African and African-American Studies, Director of the W.E.B. Du Bois Institute for African and African-American Research, Harvard University.*

Dr. Henry Louis Gates, Jr., Series Advisor

Dr. Henry Louis Gates, Jr., is author of a number of books including: *The Trials of Phillis Wheatley: America's First Poet and Her Encounters with the Founding Fathers*; *The African-American Century* (with Cornel West); *Little Known Black History Facts*; *Africana: The Encyclopedia of the African American Experience*; *Wonders of the African World*; *The Future of The Race* (with Cornel West); *Colored People: A Memoir*; *Loose Cannons: Notes on the Culture Wars*; *The Signifying Monkey: Towards A Theory of Afro-American Literary Criticism*; *Figures in Black: Words, Signs, and the Racial Self*; and *Thirteen Ways of Looking at a Black Man*.

Professor Gates earned his M.A. and Ph.D. in English Literature from Clare College at the University of Cambridge. Before beginning his work at Harvard in 1991, he taught at Yale, Cornell, and Duke universities. He has been named one of *Time* magazine's "25 Most Influential Americans," received a National Humanities Medal, and was elected to the American Academy of Arts and Letters.

HENRY BIBB:
ESCAPE TO FREEDOM

HENRY TRIED TO SCRAMBLE OVER THE FENCE, but his pursuers grabbed his legs and threatened to shoot him if he kept trying to run. He still kicked at them. He landed a direct blow into one man's eyes, but the crowd of men wielding clubs and guns was too much for Henry. They surrounded him and almost choked him to death. Then, they dragged him down the streets of Cincinnati, Ohio, to the justice office. But as Henry would write later, "It was more like an office of injustice."[1] It was 1838, and Henry Bibb was a runaway slave and he was being taken back to the plantation of William Gatewood—located in the slave state of Kentucky.

Born a Slave
Henry Bibb was born in 1815, the eldest son of a slave and her owner. He never knew his father because

Henry was sold and taken away from his mother when he was very young. His life was filled with backbreaking work and little rest. Like most slaves, he worked from very early in the morning until late at night. He was always hungry because there was never enough to eat. When he did finally get to lie down, his bed was a cold bench without even a blanket to cover him.[2] If he protested his harsh treatment in any way, Henry would feel the whip against his small back by the overseer, a white man who ran the plantation for the owner.

Henry decided, when he was ten years old, to try and run away to freedom in the North every chance he got. Henry had talked about the North with other slaves and overheard whites talking among themselves. He said, "I learned the art of running away to perfection. I made a regular business of it, and never gave it up until I had broken the

Before becoming a free man, Henry Bibb had been oppressed on a slave plantation.

bands of slavery, and landed myself safely in Canada, where I was regarded as a man, and not as a thing."[3]

Running Away From Slavery

For a young slave boy or girl, dreaming of freedom was a dangerous thing because trying to escape could mean death. Most slaves did not know the geography outside their plantation. They had no means of transportation, because a slave could not get on a boat or a train without permission papers from his or her owner. Many had to cross unfamiliar swamps or rivers. Travel was mostly done at night. Runaway slaves had little money or food. An escaped slave was always on the lookout for people likely to betray him or her to the local authorities. Because laws were passed that forbade slaves to read and write, many slaves did not understand road signs or even a "Wanted" poster nailed to a tree by slave hunters.

Slave hunters were local bands of armed men that rode through the countryside making sure the slaves stayed on their plantations. They would beat and sometimes kill runaway slaves. On the trek northward, the frightened slave would be listening intently for the slave hunters' ferocious hounds that could tear a person to pieces. Each day might bring capture and a return to the dreaded master with his whip.[4]

Henry and Malinda

In 1833, when Henry Bibb was eighteen years old, he met a girl named Malinda. She was a slave who worked on the nearby Gatewood plantation.[5] Bibb would often leave his master's house without permission just to see Malinda. Upon returning, he would be flogged for being away without a pass. Many slaves in Antebellum America would run away for short periods of time to rejoin family that had been sold to other slaveholders. Most white owners did not care if husbands were separated from wives or mothers from their babies.[6] Bibb endured each tortured lashing until his owner, tiring of the troublesome slave, decided to give in and sell Henry Bibb to Malinda's master, William Gatewood.

Malinda and Henry wanted to marry, but slaves were not allowed to legally wed. So, they would have ceremonies on their own. Just saying out loud to everyone that they were married, made it so. Sometimes, they would even "jump the broom." A broom would be held about a foot off the floor and the couple would jump over it. Once they jumped, they were married in the eyes of the slave community.[7]

Protecting the Family

After a while, Malinda and Henry Bibb had a lovely daughter named Mary Frances. They were fairly happy

During a "jump the broom" wedding ceremony, the man and woman both jumped at the same time.

until Henry realized that he was powerless to help his wife or his little girl whenever their masters would beat them.

One day, while Malinda and Henry were working in the fields, the mistress of the plantation beat their little girl so severely that she had a large welt on the side of her face. When Henry saw this, he knew he had to try and escape and then later bring his family to freedom. He wrote, "It required all the moral courage that I was master of to suppress my feeling while taking leave of my little family."[8]

SOURCE DOCUMENT

The slave holders are generally rich, aristocratic, overbearing; and they look with utter contempt upon a poor laboring man, who earns his bread by the "sweat of his brow," whether he be moral or immoral, honest or dishonest. No matter whether he is white or black; if he performs manual labor for a livelihood, he is looked upon as being inferior to a slaveholder, and but little better off than the slave, who toils without wages under the lash. It is true, that the slaveholder, and non-slaveholder, are living under the same laws in the same State. But the one is rich, the other is poor; one is educated, the other is uneducated; one has houses, land and influence, the other has none. This being the case, that class of the non-slaveholders would be glad to see slavery abolished, but they dare not speak it aloud.[9]

Henry Bibb described how poor white laborers in the South secretly wanted slavery abolished.

On the Run

On Christmas in 1837, Henry Bibb got a pass from William Gatewood to try and find work nearby. Sometimes when the workload on a plantation slowed, owners would hire out some of their slaves to be employed by local businesses. They also took whatever money the slave earned.[10] Bibb used this ruse to catch a steamboat to Perrysburgh, Ohio, where he found work.[11] He worked all winter and met abolitionist friends that aided him in his desire to bring his family north. They were worried when he insisted on going back to Kentucky for his wife and daughter. His friends were sure that Gatewood would be searching for him. Henry Bibb did not listen. He was brave and he missed his family too much, so he went back in May of 1837 to get them and take them to Canada.[12]

Tricked By Slave Owners and Slave Hunters

Bibb made it back to Gatewood Plantation undetected and secretly met Malinda to give her money for steamboat passage to Cincinnati. She promised she would see him the next Sunday.[13] She did not make it. Her owners lied to her and told her that the abolitionists had promised to help her husband, but then had sold Henry to slaveholders in New Orleans. This frightened her. Slaves that were sold "down river" to Louisiana rarely escaped again. The swampy climate and working conditions were too brutal.[14]

Henry Bibb and his abolitionist friends started arranging for passage to Lake Erie for Henry's family. At this time, American abolitionists had put in place something called the Underground Railroad. It was not a railroad with trains and tracks. There were "stations," or safe houses, where runaway slaves could be hidden from the slave hunters and helped to other stations along the road to freedom in the North. Runaway slaves needed food, clothing, and money. So, the abolitionists raised money from anti-slavery groups who wanted to help.[15]

Unfortunately for Bibb, informants hired by Gatewood's slave hunters pretended they were abolitionists. They told the slave hunters where he was. He bolted and tried to climb a fence to get away. They caught him and locked him up in the local jail. Henry Bibb later wrote, "This was the first time in my life that I had been put into a jail. It was truly distressing to my feelings to be locked up in a cold dungeon for no crime."[16]

The slave hunters thought that Bibb could tell them the whereabouts of other runaway slaves. He refused, replying:

> No, gentlemen, I cannot commit or do an act of that kind
> . . . I know that I am now in the power of the master who

can sell me from my family for life, or punish me for the crime of running away . . . I also know that I have been deceived and betrayed by men who professed to be my best friends; but can all this justify me in becoming a traitor to others?[17]

A Brief Reunion

Miraculously, Henry Bibb escaped and made it secretly back to his mother and wife. His mother found someone who could hide her son. Henry Bibb wrote that, "The next day after my arrival . . . [they] came to the very house wherein I was concealed and talked in my hearing to the family about my escape . . . He was near enough for me to have laid my hands on his head while in that house."[18] Fearing that the reward for him would tempt people to turn him in, Henry Bibb told a tearful Malinda that he had to leave again and try to get to Ohio. Sadly, Bibb *was* betrayed again, by the people hiding him, for a five-dollar reward.

"Shoot him down! Shoot him down! If he offers to run or resist, kill him!" the slave hunters cried as they surrounded Henry Bibb.[19] They tied his hands behind him and robbed him of his money, a silver watch, a pocketknife, and a Bible. Then, they chained his hands and feet with heavy irons.[20] William Gatewood, master of Henry, Malinda and Mary Frances Bibb, decided to sell the entire family at the slave market.

Eventually, Henry Bibb and his family were taken to New Orleans and sold to a man named Deacon Whitfield who decided to split the family up. Henry Bibb wrote that, "This was truly heart-rending to my poor wife; the thought of our being torn apart in a strange land after having been sold away from all her friends and relations, was more than she could bear."[21]

Family on the Run

The entire family decided to escape. But the murky swamps of Louisiana were not the same as the rolling hills of Kentucky. The little family became lost in the rugged terrain along the Red River. There were snakes and alligators. They finally found themselves on a tiny island, dead tired from their ordeal. They quickly fell asleep only to be awakened in the dead of night to the howling of wolves.[22]

The beasts had surrounded the Bibbs's camp, but Henry fought them off. The family then began to travel through the woods, not sure of where they were going. Soon, the slave hunters' dogs were after them. Henry Bibb started to run with his little daughter in his arms, but he tripped and fell. Mary Frances got hurt and was bleeding very much, but she kept silent to protect her family from being discovered. But Bibb knew the running was over. "The dogs were soon at

Slave hunters often used bloodhounds to track down and chase slaves.

our heels, and we were compelled to stop or be torn to pieces by them."[23]

The next day Henry was whipped and then fitted with a heavy iron collar with a long prong extending above his head with a bell on it. He was forced to wear this heavy load of iron for six weeks and was chained to a log every night after working all day in the fields. Henry Bibb was soon sold to some gamblers. As he left with his new owners, Henry could hear the horrified screams and weeping of Malinda and Mary Frances. He would never see them again.[24]

The Fate of Henry Bibb

Many slave families in the Antebellum South were forced to live and work their entire lives at the whim of white plantation owners and their families. These men, women and children were considered property, nothing more. True to form, Henry Bibb did escape again. He taught himself to read and write, and became a member of the abolitionist movement. He lectured around the country, trying to convince people of the horror of slavery. He wrote the following at the beginning of his 1849 autobiography:

> I have been educated in the school of adversity, whips, and chains . . . to be changed from a chattel to a human being is no light matter . . . if I could reach the ears of every slave today throughout the whole continent of

America, I would teach the same lesson . . . "break your chains and fly for freedom!"[25]

African Slavery

Henry Bibb's personal story illustrates one man's viewpoint of the institution of slavery—the viewpoint of the slaves living under the domination of a harsh white society. The first slaves arrived in the British colonies by the early 1600s, and slavery did not officially end until Congress passed the Thirteenth Amendment in 1865. Slavery was the deliberate exploitation of people thought of as property. Usually, the people chosen to be slaves were people who had dark skin. Slaves would toil their entire lives to enrich others, rarely ever receiving any money for the hard work they did. Slaves were supposed to obey the owners who had purchased them.

As time went on the slave trade developed a triangular pattern. Goods were shipped from England to Africa and traded for slaves who were then taken to America or the West Indies. The slave ships would then return to England with fruits and vegetables or money. Many white people of the time felt that slavery was a good thing. Other white people were confused about it and could not make up their minds whether blacks should be given their freedom. Some people worked very hard to end slavery. They were called abolitionists and by the early 1800s they helped to end most slavery in the northern United States. The southern states refused to give up their slaves though, and this disagreement ended in a bloody Civil War between the North and the South from 1861 to 1865.

This book contains the personal stories of people who were very involved in slavery. There is one account of a slave trader, another of the daughter of a Southern slave owner. There is a tale of a slave woman who hid herself for seven years in a cramped space just to be free. Another account describes two famous abolitionists who tirelessly fought the negative attitudes held by whites toward African Americans. All of these people have a unique story to tell about slavery. All of them have views that were carefully shaped by their experiences. The institution of slavery was in place for a very long time and deeply affected the United States. The legacy of slavery is with us still today. This book is about people telling their own history as *they* see it. Keep in mind that the stories people tell themselves *about* themselves are the most powerful stories of all.

CHAPTER

JOHN NEWTON: SLAVE MERCHANT

IN 1745, WHEN JOHN NEWTON WAS TWENTY YEARS old, he found himself being treated like a slave on an island off the coast of Sierra Leone in Africa. Coming from a wealthy white English family, John could hardly believe what had happened to him. His father was an important master of ships who had hoped John would make a fine sailor someday, but Newton was a high-spirited young man who got into trouble early in his sea career. So, finally, his captain became angry enough to kick John off the ship and Newton ended up at the mercy of a white slave dealer named Clow and his African wife.[1]

As a White Slave

Newton was forced to work long hours for no pay on a lime plantation. He wrote later that his "bed was a

John Newton, a young man of privilege, soon found himself a slave on a lime plantation.

mat spread upon a board . . . and a log of wood my pillow."[2] He never had enough to eat and had to dig up roots from the ground and eat them. In the very hot and humid weather of Sierra Leone, English people died easily from the climate and diseases such as yellow fever and malaria. Newton complained that his only clothes were "a shirt, a pair of trousers, a cotton handkerchief instead of a cap."[3] It rained all day and all night, on and off, for months. Newton would feel the drops falling on his head, running down his face and into his eyes. The rain would slide inside his collar and down his neck, going through his clothes to his skin so that he never felt dry. Because of the continuous dampness, Newton became very ill and almost did not survive.[4]

The Slave Trade

His father had been looking for his long lost son and asked many captains of many ships to ask about him in all their ports of call. At last, the ship *The Greyhound* found him. John was thankful that his horrifying ordeal as someone's slave was over, but the experience did not make Newton condemn slavery. In fact, Newton became a slave trader of his own ship, the *Duke of Argyle*, in 1750 when he was twenty-five years old.

In 1750, people felt slavery was very important to the English and American economic system. Big companies like the Dutch West India Company and the English Royal African Company had investors in Europe and America who wanted to make money from selling sugar and rum, but mostly money was made from selling and transporting slaves.[5] The people who paid for the slave ships were only concerned with profiting on their original investment. They did not usually feel that buying and selling human beings whose skin was different was wrong. A small religious group called the Quakers were against slavery, but most white people accepted it without question.

Views on Africans

Of course, Newton felt enslaving Englishmen was a crime, but putting Africans in chains was just good business because much of the white world viewed Africans as less than human. On board his ship, Newton referred to his white crew as "people," while the Africans in his care were assigned numbers.[6]

According to Newton, the slaves believed in magic and witchcraft. He did not understand that African religions and African gods were very different than the beliefs he was taught as a child. All sea captains had to keep a daily journal during each voyage and, one day in 1753, Newton wrote:

> The three greatest blessings of which human nature is capable are . . . religion, liberty and love. In each of these how highly has God distinguished me! But here in Africa are whole nations around me, whose languages . . . have no words among them . . . [for] these engaging ideas.[7]

The Triangular Trade

To Newton and the other slave traders of the day African people were just cargo to be taken across the sea to be sold in the Triangular Trade. One side of the triangle was the trip from England to the West Coast of Africa. Ships carried cargoes of cloth, guns, alcohol and other items that the English knew the local African slave dealers would like to have. When the ships arrived, they cast off their longboats to sail up and down the coast along many rivers and creeks seeking slaves to buy. This was called the "coasting period," and the trading often lasted six to eight months. The second side of the triangle was called the "Middle Passage" between Africa and North America. This trip took about two months, depending on the

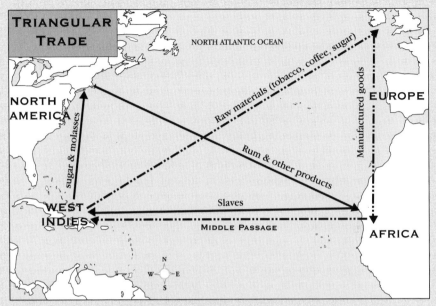

The Triangular Trade took on different forms. However, each version involved the dreaded Middle Passage.

weather. When they reached North America, the slaves were sold to white plantation owners. The last side of the triangle was the homeward trip back to England. The ship sometimes carried cotton, sugar, or rum. However, money was the chief cargo and it was not in the cargo hold, but lined the pockets of the captain and the slave ship's owners.[8] When the slave trade was going strongest in the 1700s, about 6 million Africans were taken across the Atlantic Ocean. Over fifty-four thousand voyages were made in three hundred years of slave trading.[9]

Life in the Slave Hold

A slave trader's most important goal was getting as many living slaves to America as possible. So men, women and children were packed very close to one another below decks. They were unable to stand erect or even sit up and had to lie on their sides.[10] Because captains were constantly afraid of slaves rising up against them, which happened quite often, the male slaves were kept under heavy guard and in chains most of the time. The women and children were also frequently chained to prevent them from throwing themselves overboard. John Newton wrote of the space allotted on his ships for the slaves:

Often, many slaves were packed into the hold of a slave ship.

The space between decks was five feet. . . . The slaves were chained in couples, right hand and right foot of one to the left of the other and so stowed upon the platform and the deck below—their headroom being rather less than thirty inches.[11]

If a slave was put on the ship at the beginning of the coasting period, it is possible that he or she could spend eight months on board a ship with very little chance to walk around freely and feel the sun on his or her face. The place below decks was always dirty from so many people living in such a small place cooped up like prisoners or animals. Newton felt that some people died of sadness. He wrote in his journal,

Wednesday 9th January . . . This day buried a fine woman slave. No. 11, having been ailing some time, but never thought her in danger till within these last 2 days; she was taken with a lethargick [sic] disorder, which they seldom recover from.[12]

Newton gave all his slaves a number to show when he bought them from the dealers on the coast of Africa. He did not use their names. Because of this, it is possible to find out when he bought No. 11. It was on the 19th of the previous November that Newton "bought a woman and a slave girl" (No. 11 and No. 12).[13] This means that No. 11 had been a captive on the *Duke of Argyle* for 51 days. Newton's ship did not leave the coast of Africa until May when he had filled his hold with at least two hundred and fifty slaves, so the slaves purchased early in the "coasting period" had been mostly chained up in his hold for six months.

Dying a Slave

Many slaves died as a result of the miserable conditions during the "Middle Passage" to America. In rough seas, the small windows, called portholes, that gave fresh air to the hold where the Africans were crowded

SOURCE DOCUMENT

If the slaves and their rooms can be constantly aired, and they are not detained too long on board, perhaps there are not many who die; but the contrary is often their lot. They are kept down, by the weather, to breathe a hot and corrupted air, sometimes for a week: this added to the galling of their irons, and the despondency which seizes their spirits when thus confined, soon becomes fatal. And every morning, perhaps, more instances than one are found, of the living and the dead, . . . [14]

In *Thoughts Upon the African Slave Trade,* John Newton describes how the horrible conditions below a slave ship's deck often proved fatal for the African captives.

together would be closed tight. It then became very hot, and many people died because they lacked air. Most of the slaves suffered from sea sickness (since they had never been on a ship) and they would vomit on the floor which would not be cleaned for days. Others died from a disease which came from these filthy conditions; a sickness Captain Newton called the "bloody flux." This illness made the slave area very dirty and caused even more people to become sick.

Between the slave dealers in the interior of Africa and the slave traders buying Africans on the coast and taking them to the other side of the ocean, the death toll was frighteningly high. Of 100 people kidnapped inside Africa and sold to slave dealers, 57 would reach the coast to be bought by slave traders and board the ships. About 51 of the 57 who survived the trip over land would make it across the ocean. Only about 48 would eventually be sold in the New World.[15] Less than half of the initial 100 people would ever make it.

Newton's Change of Heart

John Newton would make three voyages as a slave trader, which was about average for a slave ship captain. Later, he would write, "my heart now shudders"[16] at the fact that he was involved in buying and selling human beings. Unlike nearly all of the slave traders,

John Newton grew to realize that slavery was wrong. He wrote "What I did, I did ignorantly."[17]

This kind of blindness to the cruelty of slavery by white people was very common. If people are always told that someone who is different is not human like themselves, they will come to believe it. If they are told this over and over again by their parents and teachers and read it in books, they will come to accept it as truth. Captain John Newton was one of the few slave traders who finally understood that just because everyone says something is right and good, does not necessarily make it so. Later, he became a priest for the Church of England and wrote many hymns, including the famous song "Amazing Grace," which is still sung today. The first verse tells the story of how someone can come to see things in a different light:

Amazing Grace, how sweet the sound
That saved a wretch like me
I once was lost, but now I'm found
Was blind, but now I see.

In 1755, John Newton gave up the slave trade for good. That same year, eleven-year-old Olaudah Equiano was taken from his home by Africans bent on selling him to Europeans on the coast. In the next story, the Middle Passage is seen through the eyes of a young African boy.

OLAUDAH EQUIANO: GOODBYE TO AFRICA

TEN YEAR OLD OLAUDAH EQUIANO DELIGHTED living in the home he called Essaka[1] in the kingdom of Benin which is now known as south-eastern Nigeria. He was a young Ibo boy who loved playing games with his brothers and his sister. He was good at hunting and enjoyed helping his father and mother tend their fields of yams, beans, and corn.[2] What was even more fun for him was celebrating the harvest with the whole village when the crops were ripe and freshly picked. Their supreme god Chukwu protected them, and his tribe was very grateful for the blessings that each year brought.[3] Olaudah wrote in his autobiography many years later about the joy of the celebration,

> We are almost a nation of dancers, musicians and poets . . . every great event . . . is celebrated in public dances which are accompanied with songs and music. . . . We

have many musical instruments, particularly drums of different kinds, . . . [something] which resembles a guitar[4] . . . and another much like a stickado.[5]

Stories of Slavery

Slavery was not unknown to Olaudah Equiano. His father was an elder, an important man in the village, and owned slaves. In Ibo villages, there was no single king that ruled everyone. Decisions were made by councils of elders, a council of chiefs, women's groups, and secret societies.[6] The chief men of the Ibo tribe acted like judges to decide arguments among the people and punishments for criminals. One sentence for breaking the law was that the person could be sold to a neighboring tribe.[7]

In Africa, slavery was thought to be serving others for a time. People felt it was more humane than jailing someone for many years or killing them.[8] The person who was enslaved would not be sent so far away from home that he or she never saw their family again. They were not treated as if they were not human. Many times, the slaves were adopted into their master's family. Lastly, they were not made slaves for life. Olaudah wrote in his book, "With us they do no more work than other members of the community, even their master . . . their food, clothing and lodging were nearly the same as theirs. . . . Some of these slaves have even slaves

Olaudah Equiano

under them, as their own property, and for their own use."[9]

Kidnapped!

One day when Olaudah and his sister were left at home alone, two men and a woman got over the walls of their yard and seized them. "Without giving us time to cry out . . . they stopped our mouths and tied our hands and ran off with us."[10] Olaudah was taken from the interior of Africa and he was sold over and over again to different families who treated him well, but he was homesick. Olaudah had never been far away from home before.

He saw many strange and some pleasant things along the way, but when he came to a big river filled with canoes he was very afraid.

> I had never before seen any water larger than a pond . . . and my surprise was mingled with no small fear when I was put into one of theses canoes. . . . I continued to travel . . . through different countries and various nations, till at the end of six or seven months after I had been kidnapped. I arrived at the seacoast.[11]

The Slave Traders

The first thing that Olaudah saw when he reached the coast was the vast ocean and a huge slave ship at anchor. The sight must have made him feel very small.

He was grabbed and dragged on board by white men. Olaudah thought they were going to kill him.[12] The crew of the slave ship spoke in a language Olaudah had never heard. He did not understand what they were trying to tell him to do. He was pushed and shoved. Worst of all, they were very dirty and stinky. Olaudah had never seen people like this. His people were very clean and washed their hands before every meal. These men smelled of liquor and body odor.

> When I looked round the ship . . . and saw . . . a multitude of black people of every description chained

Some Africans sold their own people to European slave traders.

SOURCE DOCUMENT

There was a very clever and decent free young mulatto-man who sailed a long time with us: he had a free woman for his wife, by whom he had a child; and she was then living on shore, . . . all knew this young man from a child that he was always free, and no one had ever claimed him as their property: however, . . . a Bermudas captain, . . . came on board of us, and seeing the mulattoman, . . . told him he was not free, and that he had orders from his master to bring him to Bermudas. The poor man could not believe the captain to be in earnest; but he was very soon undeceived, his men laying violent hands on him: and although he shewed a certificate of his being born free in St. Kitt's, . . . he was taken forcibly out of our vessel. . . . the next day, without . . . or suffering him even to see his wife or child, he was carried away , and probably doomed never more in this world to see them again.[13]

Olaudah Equiano describes how a free black man was forced into slavery by a captain of a slaver.

together, every one of their [faces] expressing . . . sorrow, I no longer doubted of my fate . . . I fell motionless on the deck and fainted.[14]

When Olaudah awoke he asked some slaves around him, "Are we not to be eaten by those white men with the horrible looks, red faces, and long hair?"[15] They told him no. They told him the white men would be taking him to work in the white man's land across the sea. What Olaudah did not know at this point was that he was about to voyage on the dreaded Middle Passage. He did not know about a land this far away from his home. He did not know that little boys like him were prized possessions of the slave traders. Boys like Olaudah were considered old enough to work like grown-ups and young enough to easily learn English. Young slaves were worth a lot of money. Proof of this would be seen many years later when the wreckage of the slave ship, the *Henrietta Marie*, would be brought up from the bottom of the ocean and one hundred pairs of shackles or handcuffs were found. They were forged just big enough for the wrists and ankles of children.[16]

Below Deck

Olaudah sank into despair because he knew that he had lost any chance of returning to Africa. Olaudah was a scared little boy. His family was gone. He was

alone. He could not understand what was being said to him or talk to the people in charge of him. New sights and smells were all around him that filled him with terror.

Olaudah was soon dragged below the ship's deck. The little boy was revolted by the stench that came up from the slave quarters and horrified by the cries of the people who were chained down there. "I became so sick and low that I was not able to eat, nor had I the least desire to taste anything. I now wished for the last friend, Death, to relieve me."[17] Terribly sad and wishing to die, Olaudah refused to eat. This angered the slave ship's crew. To them, this young boy was worth too much money to let him starve himself. So they held him by the hands, laid him over a big crank on the ship, tied his feet and whipped him until he screamed. Olaudah wrote later that, even though he was very afraid of the water, if he could have gotten over the ropes on the sides of the ship, "I would have jumped over the side."[18]

Because the ship was in its coasting period and Olaudah was a young boy, he was allowed to stay on deck in the fresh air most of the time. His captors did not see him as a threat. When the ship finally set sail for the Middle Passage, Olaudah was once again put down below decks.

> The closeness of the place, and the heat of the climate, added to the number in the ship, which was so crowded that each had scarcely room to turn himself, almost suffocated us . . . the shrieks of the women, and the groans of the dying tendered the whole a scene of horror almost inconceiveable [sic].[19]

Immense Suffering

Olaudah was confined tightly like this because the Europeans tried to take as many slaves with them to sell in the New World as they could. Many slaves died during the trip, so the slave traders would cram too many people into the hold to make up for the ones who would eventually die. This caused much suffering and even more death.

To try and keep the adult slaves alive, the crew would also bring them up on deck for short periods of time. Olaudah was able to see some of what the other slaves endured. Many wanted to starve themselves, and he saw the slaves whipped for not eating. Other times, lips would be burned with a hot coal or molten lead would be poured on the skin to force the slaves to eat.[20] One day, Olaudah witnessed a suicide.

> . . . We had a smooth sea . . . two of my wearied countrymen, who were chained together (I was near them at the

Slaves on ships were often whipped for not eating. Once they reached American plantations, slaves were often whipped by the overseer. Many slaves ran away to escape this torture.

time), preferring death to such a life of misery . . . jumped into the sea . . . and I believe many more would very soon have done the same if they had not been prevented by the ship's crew.[21]

Africans aboard ship did not have many ways to resist their captors. It was just too difficult. Some tried to jump into the ocean. Others tried to take over the ship. Both types of resistance were seen as slave revolts. Both were harshly dealt with by the captains of the slave ships.

The Voyage's End

Finally, Olaudah Equiano reached the end of his voyage and his ship pulled into the harbor of the island of Barbados. When they anchored, Olaudah described how the merchants and planters immediately came on board and rushed toward the Africans. The strange men made them jump up and down to see if the slaves were healthy and poked them all over their bodies. Olaudah wrote, "And [then they] pointed to land, signifying we were to go there. We thought by this we should be eaten by these ugly men."[22] Later on, Olaudah and the other slaves were sold in the marketplace. In his autobiography, Olaudah described the sale and called it "the scramble," with loved ones and relatives being separated, never to see each other again. He later added:

On a signal given (as the beat of a drum), the buyers rush at once into the yard where the slaves are confined and make a choice of [what] they like best. The noise . . . and the eagerness visible in the [faces] of the buyers . . . increase the apprehensions of the terrified Africans. . . .[23]

In a few days, Olaudah Equiano was taken to Virginia where he was sold to a local planter. He was only there a few months when a British officer in the navy bought him and took him to England to be his aide. Olaudah would eventually fight in the French and Indian War and would later work on slave ships himself until he was able to buy his own freedom in 1766.[24]

Equiano's Story

Many European and American scientists of the time believed that the way people looked determined what they were like inside. These men thought that the color of someone's skin or the shape of someone's eyes was proof of inferiority or superiority. To them, humanity was divided into racial groups that went from higher to lower on a scale of worth. White Europeans considered themselves to be the most superior. Africans were thought to be the most inferior. Equiano, unfortunately, was an African Ibo boy.

Olaudah Equiano's story has been challenged by some historians. Some say that it is not completely true. But people telling their own personal stories usually leave out parts or put in parts that are not exactly fact. Slave stories are very special in that they give us an idea of what it must have been like to live as a slave. As one can see, Equiano's view of slavery was much different from the white Europeans of the day.

Olaudah Equiano would eventually become a leading figure in the abolitionist movement against slavery and millions would read about his life in the years to come. But he would never know what happened to his little sister or see his parents again.

JOSEPH LE CONTE:
SCIENCE AND
RACISM

JOSEPH LE CONTE WAS BORN ON A PLANTATION in Liberty County in the state of Georgia in 1823. About two hundred slaves were forced to work for Joseph and his family and, growing up, Joseph was friendly to many of them. Daddy Dick was a slave and the family gardener, who helped Joseph's father create a beautiful botanical garden filled with strange and interesting plants. Daddy Dick and Joseph's father worked closely together to create new types of plant life. People from all over the world would visit his father's garden and marvel at the wonders in it and the talents of the growers. Le Conte wrote in his autobiography that his experience in the garden as a young boy would inspire him to become a scientist later in life.[1] Joseph had been taught by his father that although Daddy Dick was intelligent, he had to be constantly supervised. This was because his skin was dark. Nearly every white person in Joseph's neighborhood and nearly every white person that he ever met felt the same way.[2]

Slave and Owner

Even though they might really like their slaves, many southern whites were comfortable telling slaves what to do, corrupting the natural give and take of normal relationships. Even a small boy or girl could totally control a slave! A boy like Joseph could beat a slave any time he felt like it and no one would say anything.

He might tell his father that a slave refused to do something. His father might then give the slave a beating. Because of this, most slaves were very careful to always smile in front of white people so they would not be mistreated. As a result, slave owners all

Joseph Le Conte held biased views on African Americans.

SOURCE DOCUMENT

But in moral character he was no less remarkable. Indeed the best qualities of character were constantly exercised and cultivated in the just, wise, and kindly management of his two hundred slaves. The negroes were strongly attached to him, and proud of calling him master.

. . . There never was a more orderly, nor apparently a happier, working class than the negroes of Liberty County as I knew them in my boyhood.[3]

In describing his father's "moral character," Joseph Le Conte depicts the slaves on their plantation and throughout the county as happy. In reality, slaves were not that happy and faked looking happy because some overseers would beat slaves if they were not smiling.

over the South started believing in a world where black people were very happy to be slaves. Joseph grew up thinking that all slaves enjoyed working hard for no pay. Le Conte described slaves, young and old, laboring to grow rice and cotton on his plantation, Woodmanston. The work lasted from early morning to late at night with very little time for rest. However, Le Conte believed that, "The negroes themselves enjoyed it hugely."[4] This idea was part of a belief system called *polygenism*.

Polygenism

Polygenism was an idea that became very popular while Joseph Le Conte was going to school, but in fact it was an old concept. One of Le Conte's teachers, Louis Agassiz, was one of polygenism's chief backers in America. This belief system basically held that a divine being had created each group on earth separately and that instead of one human race, there were three: whites, Asians and blacks. Many scientists thought that the physical differences in people were directly connected to their intelligence and ability. For example, since Asians had eyes that looked slanted and they appeared to be looking out of the corner of their eyes, they were considered to be sneaky and tricky.[5] Some people believed that certain groups were better than other ones and that God had ranked the groups in a special order of value from highest to lowest. Many scientists called it "The Great Chain of Being." According to many white people in the 1800s, Asians, Hispanics, American Indians, Africans and all the other people with darker skin were considered inferior to whites.

When slave trading began in the seventeenth century, white Europeans tended to view Africans as a separate kind of person. Differences in people were seen in religious terms. White people believed that the divine being had chosen whites to lead and control the world because they were "good." Many Europeans felt that since Africans were not like them and they did not believe in the same god, they could be treated like animals.[6] Even Joseph Le Conte, who said he treated all his slaves well, wrote that the planters in his neighborhood "formed themselves into a mounted police that regularly patrolled the country by night" in order to capture and arrest slaves trying to escape. Because of this harsh control, Le Conte wrote, "There never was a more orderly, nor apparently happier, working class than the negroes of Liberty County."[7]

Even President Thomas Jefferson thought black people were inferior to whites. This founder, who wrote the Declaration of Independence and who believed in equality and freedom, did not believe that these rights were meant for black people too. Jefferson hated slavery, even though he owned over two hundred slaves. But he most hated slavery for how it affected white children. He felt it made white children very comfortable with tyranny, cruelty, and oppression over others. Jefferson wrote in his *Notes on Virginia* about how children react when they see their parents losing their temper with a slave. "Our children see this and learn to imitate it . . . the parent storms, the child looks on . . . [and] puts on the same airs in the circle of smaller slaves, gives loose to his worst of passions and thus is nursed, educated, and daily exercised in tyranny. . . ."[8] However, Jefferson stuck to the belief that black people were childlike and lacked the intelligence of whites. In a letter to a friend, Jefferson dismissed the famous African-American poet Phillis Wheatley writing, "Misery is often the parent of the most affecting touches in poetry—Among blacks is misery enough, God knows, but not poetry."[9]

Paternalism

Later in his life, Joseph Le Conte would write about why it was important that white Southerners keep black people in slavery. Le Conte saw his use of slaves as very moral and that his "burden" was to spend his life selflessly taking care of his slaves. In reality, Le Conte's slaves were taking care of him and his family by doing all the work on the farm. Many Southerners felt the same way as Le Conte. They saw slave ownership as a good thing because they felt that African Americans could not take care of themselves and needed white people to guide and help them become "civilized." Le Conte wrote:

> Not only has the Negro been elevated to his present condition by contact with the white race, but he is sustained in that position . . . by the same contact, and

Phillis Wheatley's *Poems on Various Subjects, Religious and Moral* was published in England and reflected her strong religious views.

whenever that support is withdrawn he [reverts] again to his primitive state. The Negro race is still in childhood; it has not yet learned to walk alone in the paths of civilization.[10]

What went hand in hand with this belief system was a philosophy called "paternalism."[11] This was the view that Southern planters should keep order and authority on their land at all times by insisting on complete obedience from the slaves. The odd part was that slaves were supposed to feel gratitude and love for their masters in return.[12]

Being Servile and Happy

The Southern planters felt that because the slaves were dependent on them for food and shelter, they should be happy and content to serve in the fields. (The slaves were only dependent because their masters refused to allow them to provide food and shelter for themselves.) The planters made the slaves bow to them all the time. The slaves had to always stand when white people came into a room and keep standing for hours until they left. They had to endure whippings from the master's children. A slave could be kicked for walking between two whites on the street.[13] Slave owners also insisted that their slaves show no signs of unhappiness. Slave Henry Watson said, "The slaveholder watches every move of the slave, and if he is downcast or sad—in fact, if they are in any mood but laughing and singing . . . they are said to have the devil in them. . . ."[14]

The idea of happy slaves made Southerners feel better about themselves. But as the 1700s turned into the 1800s, more people started speaking out against slavery. They even started calling the slave owners "evil." More Southern planters felt threatened and they decided to defend their way of life. So the happy and contented slave became a comfortable myth that the planters clung to. People wrote books, drew pictures and composed songs about "happy" slaves. Southerners did not want to think of themselves as bad people. Myths come in very handy when groups of people do not want to face things they are doing or have done. What shattered the myth and the Southern way of life was the American Civil War.

On the Run

Joseph Le Conte describes how he was almost captured by the Yankees during the war in his autobiography. Northern Army General Sherman and his men were moving through the Georgia countryside, rounding up all the Southern men they could find. They were looking for Joseph. He was trying to escape any way he could and he recalled how earnestly his former slaves helped him run away.

Southern slave owners wanted other whites to believe that slaves were happy with their lives.

I paid one of my negroes twenty dollars to carry my boys back home . . . shook each heartily by the hand and bade them goodbye. 'Goodbye, Massah,[15] and God bless you!' 'I hope the Lord will keep you from them Yankees, dear Massah!'—such were the parting words that greeted me . . . Were they sincere?[16]

Even Joseph Le Conte, so outwardly sure of his slave's love for him, still had doubts. He should have doubted. The reason why his slaves were anxious to see him go was because they had taken some of Le Conte's property and were leaving with the permission of the Yankee troops. They were finally free! Frederick Douglass, the great black abolitionist, wrote that slaves "stealing" from their masters was moral and just: "Considering that my labor and person were the property of [my master] and that I was by him deprived of the necessaries of life—necessaries obtained by my own labor—it was easy to deduce the right to supply myself with what was my own."[17]

What Le Conte Did Not Know

Le Conte and many other planters failed to see that slaves often wore false faces to their masters. Any group who is under the control of another group will do this for self-preservation. The oppressed group will develop code words that their oppressors do not know, in order to communicate among themselves.

They will also resist slavery in ways that create doubts in the master's mind, but do not bring on a whipping. These acts of resistance can be small, but they are effective. A slave might take longer to complete a task. A slave might fake confusion on

how to do a job, forcing the master to do it himself. A machine might be accidentally broken or a chicken stolen for extra food for the underfed slave family. These acts of resistance gave the slaveholders the idea that slaves were mentally slow and that they liked to steal. But that is only because the slave owners could not bring themselves to believe the reality of the tyranny in which they were active participants.[18] Their slaves hated slavery and many felt the planters had stolen their very *lives* from them.

Le Conte After the War

Joseph Le Conte lived to a very old age still believing in polygenism. Along with many white Southerners, Le Conte worked very hard to deny blacks the right to vote after the war. He believed that former slaves would never be as smart as whites, so only whites should rule America. Le Conte wrote, "The Negro race as a whole is certainly at present . . . unworthy of the ballot. The South . . . is solid for self-government by the white race as the only self-governing race."[19] This terrible deed was not legally undone until the Voting Rights Act in 1964 after many years of struggle.

Unlike slave-owning men who commanded absolute obedience from their slaves and family, the experience of white women under paternalism was quite different. Most Southern women willingly yielded control to their fathers and husbands. For them, the presence of slaves in the home was seen as a natural result of Southern kindness toward people less "civilized." People running this way and that, doing anything a white person wanted, was the accepted order of things. Viewing slavery from this vantage point, many women felt that their relationships with their slaves were quite pleasant and caring. Lots of young ladies like Letitia Burwell were offended when Northerners put down their way of life.

CHAPTER

LETITIA BURWELL: PAMPERED BLINDNESS

AFTER THE CIVIL WAR, MANY SOUTHERN SLAVE owners were surprised that a lot of people thought of them as "inhuman" or "dealers of human souls." Some were astonished that their grand and graceful lives were seen in such harsh, unforgiving terms. One of them, Letitia M. Burwell, wealthy granddaughter of a governor, decided to set the record straight. She wrote a story of her times as a young girl growing up on a Virginia plantation and her visits to other plantations in the neighboring region. Letitia felt that every single one of the slave owners she met were just and good people. In her opinion, she had never seen a slave abused or mistreated. She wrote that she could not believe that she was "descended from such monsters," and she wanted people to know what she felt was the truth about the people who owned slaves—the "noble men and virtuous women who have passed away."[1]

Letitia Thought the Slaves Were Happy

According to Letitia, the Burwell plantation was comfortable, calm, and beautiful. Slave cabins were gaily painted white and had delicious vegetable gardens next to them. Whenever the slaves were hungry they could just pick food off the nearby trees. The male slaves sang joyfully while they worked in the fields and the women happily did their sewing, weaving, and housecleaning while their children romped and played in the yard. She wrote, "These formed the only pictures familiar to my childhood . . . all were merryhearted, and among them I never saw a discontented [unhappy] face."[2]

The Southern Culture

Like most daughters of Southern plantation owners, Letitia grew up in the country and did not have much contact with big cities. She did not join women's groups or become active in political clubs like some women in the North. In Southern culture, such activities were not considered ladylike. Letitia was only taught to manage a slave household ruled strictly, by

Letitia Burwell sits with a slave at her feet. Burwell thought that her slaves were happy with their situation. However, every day slaves ran away from plantations in the South to seek a better life in the North.

her father first and then later her husband. Southern women and men believed in the idea of paternalism—a white man ruling the plantation and the people on it (both black and white) with an iron hand.[3] A lady was supposed to agree with the men around her no matter what she really thought. Most important, Letitia was brought up assuming that her most common needs would be met by the everyday efforts of slaves.[4]

Life in the "Big House"

Letitia Burwell called her servants "indispensables" and wrote that her family had many. Her mother chose certain slaves, at ages ten or twelve, to work in the family home which was called the "Big House." Older house slaves would teach them about cleaning and cooking, everything about serving the plantation family. Burwell wrote "they might be seen constantly darting about on errands from the house to the kitchen and the cabins, upstairs and downstairs." It was common for young house slaves to sleep on bedroom floors so they could get up and serve their mistress or master in the middle of the night. Letitia really believed that the slaves enjoyed this and wrote, "These black, smiling 'indispensables' . . . insisted so good naturedly on . . . combing [my] hair, pulling off [my] slippers—that one had not the heart to refuse."[5]

Usually older children in most families have certain

Here, a house slave fans a group of whites. House slaves worked for the comfort of plantation-owning families and were constantly under their watchful eyes.

chores like taking out the trash or washing the dishes. Daughters of slaveholders did not have much of anything to do. They might take care of their own rooms a little and maybe pick some pretty flowers for decorating, but most of their time was spent visiting friends, shopping, and fixing their hair.[6] Letitia

Burwell wrote, "One easily acquired a habit of being waited upon, there being so many servants with so little to do. It was natural to ask for a drink of water when the water was right at hand, and to have things brought which you might easily have gotten yourself." Letitia said the slaves were "so pleased" at serving her and her friends that she never hesitated to ask them to do the simplest things.[7]

Slaves did mostly everything for the plantation family. Many young white girls grew up not knowing how to care for their own children because it was assumed a slave would do it. Slave cooks prepared all the meals; so many young women never knew how to cook. House servants cleaned the house, made clothes, wove rugs, and hung drapes. Plantation girls never were taught how to do any of the things they might need to do for themselves. Interestingly, the mistress of a plantation would take credit for work she had not done herself. For example, in letters that were written at the time, some young women would complain to friends that they had been ironing clothes all day. Actually, the women had only been seeing to it that their slaves ironed the clothes.[8] Most slaveholding women never touched a hot iron or a wrinkled blouse.

Though house slaves sometimes had more privileges than field slaves, they were still subjected to much hard work.

The Slave/Mistress Relationship

Although it was very hard to be a house slave, many mistresses and servants became strongly tied to one another. Just by seeing each other day after day, slaves and their owners sometimes became very close emotionally. Many times the slave nurses had raised their masters and mistresses from the time they were babies. The white children grew up to love their nurses like mothers. The slaves also knew the most intimate secrets of the white young ladies they served. Slaves needed the protection a mistress could give them from needless hardship or to escape punishment from the master. Both black women and white women were dependent on each other for certain personal freedoms, and they worked together to achieve them.[9]

Sometimes the slave and her mistress would become lifelong friends. Letitia Burwell wrote that on the Virginian Otterburn plantation, whenever the master and mistress left, they gave the keys to a particular slave to manage the place. "No more sincere attachment could have existed than that between this lady and her servant. . . . When the [servant] was seized with a contagious fever which ended her life, she could not have had a more faithful friend and nurse than was her mistress."[10]

Slave Power

House slaves could also gain much power by using their wits. These slaves got favors from their masters and mistresses because they were just better at running the plantation than their owners were. Burwell told a story of Aunt Fanny, a cook on the plantation of a famous lawyer:

> Although considered the owner of his house, it was a mistake. . . . This gentlemen had no 'rights' there whatever . . . his house being under the entire command of Aunt Fanny . . . a huge mulatto woman whose word was law and whose voice thundered abuse if any dared to disobey her.[11]

Aunt Fanny even started her own business. While cooking for the family, she would make her own popular "butter soap." One time her owner pleaded with her to stop boiling soap because it was costing him a small fortune in firewood. And Aunt Fanny "looking at him with astonishment, but with firmness in her eye," replied, "Couldn't possibly do it . . . because soap, sir, soap's my maintenance!"[12] Aunt Fanny was a smart and enterprising person who demanded respect from her owners. The soap business was *her* business and she knew her particular owner would not deprive

SOURCE DOCUMENT

Her room was crowded with negroes who had come to perform their religious rites around the deathbed. Joining hands, they performed a savage dance, shouting wildly around her bed. This was horrible to hear and see especially as in this family every effort had been made to instruct their negro dependents in the truths of religion; . . . But although an intelligent woman, she seemed to cling to the superstitions of her race.

. . . the friend and minister of the family . . . marked some passages in the Bible, and asked me to go and read them to her. I went, and said to her: "Aunt Fanny, here are some verses Mr. Mitchell has marked for me to read to you, . . ." Then said I: "We are afraid the noise and dancing have made you worse."

Speaking feebly, she replied: "Honey, dat kind o' 'ligion suit us black folks better 'an yo' kind. What suit Mars' Charles mind karn't suit mine."[13]

Letitita Burwell describes the death of a house slave, Aunt Fanny. Burwell does not understand or accept the slaves' religion and tries to force her own religion on Aunt Fanny while she is on her deathbed.

her of it because he had grown to depend on her completely.

Letitia Burwell's Final Word

With the coming of the Civil War, many rich young Southern women got a small taste of what it was like to do something besides fix their hair for parties! They had to learn many everyday tasks to support themselves and their families. Still, there were many who never got over the loss of the Southern plantation style of living. Many felt that Southern slave owners had given up *their* freedom to devote themselves to the well-being of their slaves. Letitia Burwell wrote that all of her ancestors made sacrifices for the family's slaves. She seemed to feel that the slaves owed her and her family for helping " . . . the naked, savage Africans to the condition of good cooks and respectable maids!"[14]

While most wealthy Southern women were being waited on hand and foot by servants, Southern black women were anxious to be free. The story of Harriet Jacobs gives another view of what life was like in the "Big House." Instead of feeling grateful, Jacobs burned with resentment. Even though paternalism limited opportunities for white women in the South, it could mean death for black female slaves. Harriet Jacobs spent almost a lifetime running away from a cruel slave owner.

HARRIET JACOBS: DESPERATE TO LIVE FREE

THE ROOM WAS SMALL. IT HAD BEEN BUILT over a shed next to her grandmother's house. Nothing had ever been in it except for rats and mice. The area was nine feet long and seven feet wide. It sloped down like a roof and its highest part was three feet. There were no windows so little air or sunlight ever got in. The space was stifling, the darkness total.[1] This is how escaped slave Harriet Jacobs would live for years. She would see the seasons change through small holes she had bored in the wood of her hiding place. Many times she would wish just once to come out and play with her two children laughing below her. She could not tell them where she was. It was too dangerous because her master, Dr. Flint, was searching for her and someone might see her and turn her in to

Harriet Jacobs dealt with a lot of strife.

the authorities. Jacobs wrote that even as hard as living in this confined room was, she "would have chosen this, rather than my lot as a slave, though white people considered it an easy one; [as] compared with the fate of others."[2]

Born a Slave

Harriet Jacobs was born a slave in Edenton, North Carolina around 1813. She belonged to the Horniblow family who had also owned her mother and grandmother. In the South, the children of slaves were the property of the person who owned the mother, not the father,[3] so this family had owned Harriet's family for generations. By the time Harriet was a small girl, her grandmother had bought her own freedom with the money she had made baking crackers late at night after she had gotten all of her work done during the day. Her grandmother had hoped someday to buy the rest of her family.[4] It was not to be.

In her autobiography, Jacobs described a happy childhood and how she did not even know she was a slave until she was six years old. She found out when her mother died suddenly. She learned from people whispering around her that she belonged to her dead mother's mistress. Luckily for Harriet, this mistress had been a good friend to Harriet's mother. She taught Harriet to read and write. This was a rare thing since it was against the law to teach a slave to read and write in the South. The mistress did not ask Harriet to work day and night like other slave owners. Harriet would write of those days, "I would sit by her side for hours, sewing diligently, with a heart as free from care as that of any free-born white child. . . . Those were happy days—too happy to last."[5]

A Horrible Surprise

When Harriet was almost twelve years old, her mistress died. Jacobs had loved her very much and was hoping that her mistress had written in her will that, upon her death, Harriet would be freed. Harriet's friends were confident that she would be a free little girl. However, when the will was read, Harriet discovered that her mistress had given her to her five-year-old niece. Harriet was devastated. She remembered how her mistress had taught her a Bible verse—*"Thou shalt love thy neighbor as thyself."*

Harriet took that sentiment to heart upon learning it. "But I was her slave, and I suppose she did not recognize me as her neighbor."[6]

"I Felt So Desolate and Alone."

Harriet soon was taken to the home of Dr. Flint to be slave to his little daughter, Emily Flint. (Dr. Flint is the name Jacobs used in her memoirs. His real name was James Norcom.) When she arrived at her new home she encountered "cold looks, cold words, and cold treatment. . . . On my narrow bed I moaned and wept, I felt so desolate and alone."[7] In a few days, Harriet realized that Mrs. Flint was nothing like her first mistress. Instead of being filled with gentleness, Mrs. Flint had "nerves . . . so strong, that she could sit in her easy chair and see a woman whipped, till the blood trickled from every stroke of the lash."[8] If Sunday dinner was not served exactly on time, Mrs. Flint would wait until all the food had been dished out to her guests and then spit in "all the kettles and pans that had been used for cooking."[9] She would do this so the slaves would not want to eat the usual leftovers, sometimes the only food offered to the slaves.

Sexual Abuse

When Harriet turned fifteen years old things began to change drastically for the worse. This time it was not

Mrs. Flint with her little ways of tormenting her servants. This time it was Dr. Flint. He started to speak "foul words" to her. He began to ask her to touch him in places on his body that Harriet's grandmother had told her not to touch until she was married to someone she loved. Dr. Flint demanded that she allow him to touch her in her private places too. Disgusted and frightened, Harriet avoided him as much as possible. But he was her owner. She wrote, "I was compelled to live under the same roof with him—where I saw a man of forty years my senior daily violating the most sacred commandments of nature. He told me I was his property; that I must be subject to his will in all things."[10]

Black slave women experienced life much differently on the plantations than white women. Under paternalism, husbands or fathers governed the white women. These same white men ruled female slaves, too.[11] Black fathers and husbands had little say in how their wives and daughters were treated. Many times, they had to sit by and watch as the white slave owner took advantage of their loved ones. Some men struck back to defend their black women, but it was dangerous and could lead to death.

The Abuse Continues
So Harriet had to take her fate into her own hands. She defied Dr. Flint by seeking protection from a local

Field work was much more physically difficult than working in the owner's house. Slaves in the field endured hard labor under the hot sun.

white man, Mr. Sands. Over time, she had two beautiful children with him. But even as the years passed, Dr. Flint did not stop from pursuing Harriet Jacobs relentlessly. Dr. Flint threatened to send her and her children to work in the hot sun on his plantation rather than work in the coolness of his house. He threatened to sell her children away from her to punish her for running away from him. He beat her. Jacobs was frantic. She disappeared from sight and hid in a spare room of a good friend of her family, a white woman who owned slaves.[12] Jacobs thought that Dr. Flint would forget after awhile. Never.

A Victory for Harriet's Family

Dr. Flint thought Jacobs had fled to New York and went to look for her there. He put advertisements in

the paper offering money to anyone who would capture her if they saw her. He put Jacobs's brother William and her two children in jail hoping that she would come out of hiding to help them. His obsession over the years had gotten the better of him and he was in need of money to keep up the search for her.[13] A slave trader, who wanted to buy Harriet Jacobs's two children and their uncle, approached him. Dr. Flint said, "I have been reflecting upon your proposition and I have concluded to let you have the three negroes if you will pay nineteen hundred dollars."[14] Dr. Flint did not know that this particular slave trader was an agent of the children's father, Mr. Sands. In a great stroke of luck and cunning, Dr. Flint had been tricked into selling Jacobs's children to their own father. The children would be free.

When Dr. Flint found out about this brave deception, he was furious. He went to Jacobs's grandmother and said, "I shall soon have her. You need never expect to see her free. She shall be my slave as long as I live, and when I am dead she shall be the slave of my children."[15] Dr. Flint left. But Jacobs rejoiced. Her children were finally free even if she herself was not. She wrote, "Whatever slavery might do to me, it could not shackle my children . . . my little ones were saved."[16]

A Sailor in the Snaky Swamp

Unfortunately, a curious slave who kept jiggling the doorknob of Jacobs's secret room discovered her hiding place in the home of her white friend. Jacobs had to get out before she was found out, so the woman brought Jacobs a disguise. It was a sailor's outfit with

Slaves often had to hide from slave catchers in the murky swamps of the South.

a jacket and pants.[17] Jacobs could not thank her enough, but her friend kissed her on the cheek and just told her to practice walking like a sailor with her hands in her pockets. If Jacobs were discovered, they both would be in jeopardy. It was against the law for anyone to hide escaped slaves.

Jacobs was helped onto a nearby boat by friends and then stayed in a local bog called the Snaky Swamp waiting for her uncle to prepare a hiding place for her. After a horrid night of snakes and mosquitoes, Jacobs was told that a hideout had been found. She was rowed ashore and walked to her grandmother's house wearing her sailor's clothes. She even passed the father of her children on the street, but he had no idea who she was. Her friend said, "You must make the most of this walk . . . for you may not have another very soon." Jacobs thought his voice sounded sad. Later she would write that "It was kind of him to conceal from me what a dismal hole was to be my home for a long, long time."[18]

A Tiny Room

Seven years. Harriet Jacobs would be in that tiny room over her grandmother's shed for seven years. Her uncle Phillip and Aunt Nancy would pass food up to her through a trap door. Sometimes they would come up to talk to her, but never in the daytime. It was too dangerous. Jacobs could not stand in an erect position, so she crawled around the small area for exercise. It was so small and so dark. Harriet Jacobs found a way to bore holes in the wood so she could get more fresh air. She wrote, "I sat by it till late into the night, to enjoy the little whiff of air that floated in." She watched her children through those holes too. "At last I heard the merry laugh of children, and presently two sweet little faces were looking up at me, as though they knew I was there, and were conscious of the joy they imparted. How I longed to *tell* them I was there!"[19]

The Trip North

After many years of agonizing confinement, Harriet Jacobs was finally smuggled on board a boat sailing north to Philadelphia, Pennsylvania. The boat passed the Snaky Swamp and Jacobs remembered the horrible night spent there. She shuddered at the thought of the bugs and crawly things in there, but the cool evening air calmed her from thoughts of the past. As the night wore on, Jacobs could not sleep. She was too excited. Could this be really happening to her? Jacobs was on deck at the crack of dawn and for the first time in her life she saw the sun rise on free soil. She watched the sky redden and it seemed like the familiar ball of flame rose slowly and majestically out of the ocean. It made the waves sparkle "and everything caught the beautiful glow." She stood on the deck with another escaped slave named Fanny and they put their arms around each other, lost in the beauty of the day.

> Before us lay the city of strangers. We looked at each other, and [our] eyes . . . were moistened with tears. We had escaped from slavery, and we supposed ourselves to be safe from the hunters. But we were alone in the world, and we had left dear ties behind us. . . .[20]

Officially Free

In Philadelphia, the Anti-Slavery Society, a Quaker group devoted to aiding runaway slaves from the South, helped Jacobs find a place to stay and a place to work. Even though Harriet Jacobs had made it to the North, this did not mean she was safe. Legislation, passed by the United States Congress in 1850, commanded "all good citizens" who knew of escaped slaves living in the North to notify the authorities so that they could be captured and taken back down South again. It was called the Fugitive Slave Act.[21] With Dr. Flint still in pursuit, Jacobs would never feel out of harm's way. Any day she could be ripped from the freedom of the North. Even though Jacobs was reunited with her two children, she herself was still owned by the Flint family. It was not until years later, after

Harriet Jacobs found refuge in Philadelphia, Pennsylvania, after she left the South.

Dr. Flint died, that one of Jacobs's abolitionist friends would buy her freedom from the husband of a now grown up Emily Flint, Harriet's old mistress.[22]

Adding Her Story to the Abolitionist Movement

Harriet Jacobs joined the abolitionists and traveled extensively with her Quaker friend Amy Post, a white lady. They both spoke against slavery and Post urged Jacobs to write her life story. It was so difficult and the

SOURCE DOCUMENT

A clergyman who goes to the south, for the first time, has usually some feeling . . . that slavery is wrong. The slaveholder suspects this, and plays his game accordingly. He makes himself as agreeable as possible; . . . After dinner [the clergyman] walks round the premises, and sees the . . . comfortable huts of favored household slaves. . . . He asks [the slaves] if they want to be free, and they say, "O, no, massa." This is sufficient to satisfy him. He comes home . . . [and] assures people that he has been to the south, and seen slavery for himself; . . . that the slaves don't want their freedom; that they have hallelujah meetings, and other religious privileges.

What does he know of the half-starved wretches toiling from dawn till dark on the plantations? of mothers shrieking for their children, torn from their arms by slave traders? of young girls dragged down into moral filth? of pools of blood around the whipping post? of hounds trained to tear human flesh? of men screwed into cotton gins to die? The slaveholder showed him none of these things, and the slaves dared not tell of them if he had asked them.[23]

Harriet Jacobs described how religious leaders from the North were often fooled by Southern slaveholders.

experience of writing brought back such painful memories, Harriet Jacobs distanced herself from the tale. She used a fictitious name, "Linda Brent," instead of her real name because she was embarrassed by some of the things she had done in her life. However, slavery forced many people to make choices they never would have made on their own in a free and just society. Desperate times can often lead people to desperate behavior. Harriet Jacobs was no different. So she gathered her courage and set down her journey to freedom on paper. She has left behind, for the world to appreciate, an unbelievable and amazing account of one woman's survival and personal strength.

When Jacobs reached Philadelphia, she discovered a whole support network devoted to runaway slaves who wanted to make new lives for themselves. Two men were very influential in that network—William Lloyd Garrison, a white man, and Frederick Douglass, an African-American man. The publication of Garrison's newspaper *The Liberator* would mark the beginning of the abolitionist movement. Douglass would inspire generations after him to seek justice and freedom for all.

Douglass and Garrison: Down With Slavery

So profoundly ignorant of the nature of slavery are many persons, that they are stubbornly incredulous whenever they read or listen to any recital of the cruelties which are daily inflicted on its victims. They do not deny that the slaves are held as property; but that terrible fact seems to convey to their minds no idea of injustice, exposure to outrage, or savage barbarity. —*Frederick Douglass*[1]

On this subject [slavery], I do not wish to think, or speak, or write, with moderation. No! no! . . . I am in earnest— I will not equivocate—I will not excuse—I will not retreat a single inch—AND I WILL BE HEARD.
—*William Lloyd Garrison*[2]

Two men challenged the people of our nation to examine how they justified to themselves that some fellow citizens were legally being bought and sold like livestock. Freedom, the most basic value and individual right, was being regularly denied to many Americans in the United States. One of these men was a former slave. His name was Frederick Douglass. The other man was William Lloyd Garrison, the son of a merchant seaman from Massachusetts.

Different Lives, Conflicting Views

Douglass had grown up owned by the Auld family. Sophie Auld, his owner's wife, had begun to teach him to read, but her husband threatened her and put a stop to it immediately. From then on, Douglass figured that if whites were that afraid of slaves reading and writing, he would teach himself. He carried a Webster's pocket spelling book with him wherever he went and learned from the white boys he played with on the Baltimore streets.[3]

Garrison's father deserted him and his family and young William was forced to work selling homemade molasses candy and firewood. As a young man, he would apprentice on a newspaper as a writer and editor. Later he published and edited this country's most influential abolitionist newspaper—*The Liberator.*[4]

These individuals were two of the most influential abolitionist figures in the United States in the decades leading up to the Civil War. They believed in freedom for the slaves, but they disagreed on how to go about making that happen. Both of these men had a strong

SOURCE DOCUMENT

. . . slaves, when inquired of as to their condition and the character of their masters, almost universally say they are contented, and that their masters are kind. The slaveholders have been known to send in spies among their slaves, to ascertain their views and feelings in regard to their condition. The frequency of this has had the effect to establish among the slaves the maxim, that a still tongue makes a wise head. They suppress the truth rather than take the consequences of telling it, and in so doing prove themselves a part of the human family. If they have any thing to say of their masters, it is generally in their masters' favor, especially when speaking to an untried man. I have been frequently asked, when a slave, if I had a kind master, and do not remember ever to have given a negative answer; nor did I, in pursuing this course, consider myself as uttering what was absolutely false; for I always measured the kindness of my master by the standard of kindness set up among slaveholders around us.[5]

In *Narrative of the Life of Frederick Douglass, an American Slave,* Douglass describes the reasons why slaves often said they were happy when asked.

will and a fierce intelligence. They would change a nation.

A Young African-American Abolitionist

In the beginning, Douglass was a star-struck young man, newly escaped to the North. He had disguised himself and, with the help of a friend's fake identification papers, hopped on a train out of Baltimore.[6] He became familiar with Garrison's paper, *The Liberator*, and it changed his life. "The Liberator was a paper after my own heart. It detested slavery. . . . I not only liked—I *loved* this paper, and its editor. He seemed a match for all the opponents of emancipation. . . . Every week *The Liberator* came, and every week I made myself master of its contents."[7]

It was not long before Frederick Douglass was speaking before large antislavery crowds in New England. "Young . . . and hopeful, I entered upon this new life in the full gush of unsuspecting enthusiasm. The cause was good; the men engaged in it were good; the means to attain its triumph, good. . . . Freedom must soon be given to the pining millions under ruthless bondage."[8] Week after week, Frederick Douglass would stand and speak to the people. In 1846, he told an audience: "This is American slavery: No education . . . forbidden by law to learn to read! If a mother shall teach her children to read, the law in

Frederick Douglass

Louisiana proclaims that she may be hanged by the neck. . . . Three millions of people shut out from the light of knowledge!"[9]

He was made to show the scars on his back from the repeated whippings he endured from a brutal overseer when he was a teenager. The people groaned at the scars and winced at his tales, but Frederick Douglass sensed something was wrong. He felt he was a curiosity, someone to be stared at rather than to be taken seriously. Douglass knew that being a fugitive slave lecturer was something important, but it was not enough for him to "narrate wrongs." He wanted to "*denounce* them."[10]

Garrison's Beliefs

The first issue of Garrison's *Liberator* appeared in January 1831. It was the result of an antislavery movement that had been building for a long time. The argument put forth by the New England Anti-Slavery Society (led by Garrison) had five main points:

- Slavery was against the teachings of Christianity and the universal brotherhood of man.

- Slavery contradicted the fundamental principle of American life: freedom as an individual right.

- Slavery was economically unwise since it depended on enforced labor and lacked efficiency.

William Lloyd Garrison

- The culture of the United States suffered because the master-slave relationship brought out the worst aspects of people. Random power over another tends to intoxicate and corrupt the people in power and the entire society.

- Slavery was a threat to the peace of the country since the South was arming itself because of a widespread fear of a slave uprising.[11]

Frederick Douglass agreed with all these points. By the 1850s, though, he strongly disagreed with Garrison's idea of how to end slavery. Garrison, and many abolitionists, believed wholeheartedly in moral persuasion. He felt that the only way to get Southern slave owners to free their slaves was to convince them that slavery was a sin against God. Garrison felt that the Constitution of the United States was a document that condoned slavery and, for this reason, the Union did not need to be preserved because the whole country was founded on injustice. In a speech, Garrison said, "Give us Disunion with liberty and a good conscience, rather than Union with slavery and moral degradation . . . shall we shake hands with those who buy, sell, torture, and . . . trade in human flesh! God forbid!"[12] That the North should hold "no union with slaveholders," was Garrison's principle, meaning he was not about to cooperate with Southerners. He believed you had to change people before you changed government, and his opinion was one of "non-resistance."[13] Garrison did not think that the abolitionist movement should be involved in politics and that moral purity was more important than political give and take. The South was to be shunned, in Garrison's view, until they came around to the right and moral way of thinking.[14]

A Change in Douglass

When Congress passed the Fugitive Slave Act in 1850, many black abolitionists felt that Garrison's approach was too unrealistic. Douglass felt that many white abolitionists did not understand the day-to-day reality of slaves. People were suffering under the slave system in the South. There had to be action. Too many people were hurting and being denied justice. Waiting for a total change in the Southern viewpoint was not practical at all. Maybe Garrison could wait around for years, but Douglass could not.

Frederick Douglass began to see that voting was "a legitimate and powerful means of abolishing slavery." Unlike Garrison, he thought that the Constitution was an antislavery document, which demanded the end of slavery "as a condition of its own existence."[15] Douglass was shocked by "the sentiment of the leader of the disunion forces [Garrison] . . . that if one vote

THE NORTH STAR.

ROCHESTER, JULY 28, 1848.

The Rights of Women.

One of the most interesting events of the past week, was the holding of what is technically styled a Woman's Rights Convention, at Seneca Falls. The speaking, addresses, and resolutions of this extraordinary meeting, were almost wholly conducted by women; and although they evidently felt themselves in a novel position, it is but simple justice to say, that their whole proceedings were characterized by marked ability and dignity. No one present, we think, however much he might be disposed to differ from the views advanced by the leading speakers on that occasion, will fail to give them credit for brilliant talents and excellent dispositions. In this meeting, as in other deliberative assemblies, there were frequently differences of opinion and animated discussion; but in no case was there the slightest absence of good feeling and decorum. Several interesting documents, setting forth the rights as well as the grievances of woman, were read. Among these was a declaration of sentiments, to be regarded as the basis of a grand movement for attaining all the civil, social, political and religious rights of woman. As these documents are soon to be published in pamphlet form, under the authority of a Committee of women, appointed by that meeting, we will not mar them by attempting any synopsis of their contents. We should not, however, do justice to our own convictions, or to the excellent persons connected with this infant movement, if we did not, in this connection, offer a few remarks on the general subject which the Convention met to consider, and the objects they seek to attain.

In doing so, we are not insensible that the bare mention of this truly important subject in any other than terms of contemptuous ridicule and scornful disfavor, is likely to excite against us the fury of bigotry and the folly of prejudice. A discussion of the rights of animals would be regarded with far more complacency by many of what are called the wise and the good of our land, than would be a discussion of the rights of woman. It is, in their estimation, to be guilty of evil thoughts, to think that woman is entitled to rights equal with man. Many who have at last made the discovery that negroes have some rights as well as other members of the human family, have yet to be convinced that woman is entitled to any. Eight years ago, a number of persons of this description actually abandoned the anti-slavery cause, lest by giving their influence in that direction, they might possibly be giving countenance to the dangerous heresy that woman, in respect to rights, stands on an equal footing with man. In the judgment of such persons, the American slave system, with all its concomitant horrors, is less to be deplored than this wicked idea. It is perhaps needless to say, that we cherish little sympathy for such sentiments, or respect for such prejudices. Standing as we do upon the watch-tower of human freedom, we cannot be deterred from an expression of our approbation of any movement, however humble, to improve and elevate the character and condition of any members of the human family. While it is impossible for us to go into this subject at length, and dispose of the various objections which are often urged against such a doctrine as that of female equality, we are free to say, that in respect to political rights, we hold woman to be justly entitled to all we claim for man. We go farther, and express our conviction that all political rights which it is expedient for man to exercise, it is equally so for woman. All that distinguishes man as an intelligent and accountable being, is equally true of woman and if that government is only just which governs by the free consent of the governed there can be no reason in the world for denying to woman the exercise of the elective franchise, or a hand in making and adminis

Frederick Douglass's newspaper the *North Star* put forth his own abolitionist views. The paper also addressed other causes such as the rights of women.

of his would emancipate every slave in this country, he would not cast that vote."[16] He was convinced that the Constitution evoked the supreme law of the land: "to form a more perfect union, establish justice, insure domestic tranquility, provide for the common defense, promote the general welfare and secure the blessings of liberty."[17] So Douglass broke with his friend William Lloyd Garrison and the two friends never reconciled. Douglass started his own newspaper, the *North Star*, to put forth his views. It was named after the star that led slaves North to freedom on the Underground Railroad.

"Three Kinds of Abolitionists"

Six years before the start of the Civil War, Douglass wrote an essay describing "Three Kinds of Abolitionists." In it, he outlined his feelings about the state of the antislavery movement. He saw the differences between Republican Party (at this time the Republican Party was brand new), Garrisonian Abolitionists and Radical Abolitionists.[18]

The Republican Party was also called the Free Soil Party because they believed that slavery should not be extended outside the South. Its motto was "No Slavery Outside the Slave States." It is important to remember that the United States was quickly establishing new territories and the Republicans wanted to prevent slavery from becoming a part of life there. They figured that slavery in the South would eventually end, "for lack of room and air in which to breathe."[19]

The Garrisonian Abolitionists were opposed to any political action against slavery. This included not voting. Douglass wrote: "They are in the country, but at the same time, they profess to stand outside of the Government." Frederick Douglass felt that the Garrisonians were telling slaves to fend for themselves and quoted something Garrison had written, "All the slave asks of us, is to stand out of the way . . . God will vindicate the oppressed, by the laws of justice which he has founded. . . . Stand alone, and let no cement of the Union bind the slave and he will right himself."[20] Defiantly, Douglass responded, "The idea of a slave righting himself, presupposes his ability to do so, unaided by Northern interference. O no! the slave *cannot* 'right himself' any more than an infant can grapple with a giant."[21]

The Radical Abolitionists, who had broken with the Garrison group, formed their own political party— the Liberty Party. This was the organization Douglass joined. The Liberty party believed *all* slavery was illegal because the Constitution guaranteed the blessings of liberty to *all* people. One could not wait until Southerners saw their moral error. One could not allow the Southern states to keep their slaves while denying new states that right. Slavery had to go. All of it. Douglass felt Radical Abolitionism took an ax to the root of the slavery tree. One had to "tear it up root and branch," and the only way this could be done was to keep the Union intact and push the federal government to abolish all slavery. Douglass thought Garrison was wrong. Ignoring the slave states was not an option. "By withdrawing from the Slave States, we withdraw from nearly four million Abolitionists, black and white."[22]

Anger at Abolitionists

As the abolitionist debate heated up, the Southern position regarding slavery hardened. They were digging in. The easiest way to keep curious fellow citizens from questioning the popular attitudes of their neighbors was censorship and silence.

At first, few whites in the country talked about slavery. People were afraid of what debate would bring. A lot of Northerners had made their family fortunes in the slave trade. Southerners had built their comfortable lifestyle on the unpaid work of slaves. When abolitionists *did* begin to talk about slavery, angry mobs would break up their meetings. People giving out antislavery newspapers were beaten in town squares. Printing presses that put out antislavery essays were destroyed. Elijah Lovejoy, an editor from

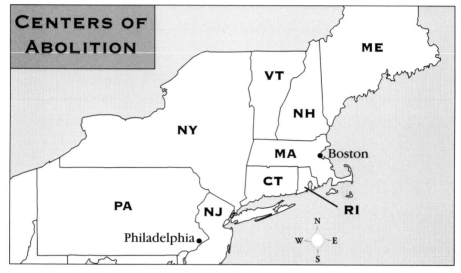

CENTERS OF ABOLITION

ME

VT

NH

NY

MA • Boston

CT

PA

NJ

RI

Philadelphia•

N
W — E
S

Boston, Massachusetts and Philadelphia, Pennsylvania were the two American cities with the most abolitionist activity.

Illinois, was murdered by a group of people while he was trying to protect his printing press.[23] In 1835, a former governor of South Carolina led a takeover of a post office and destroyed bags of antislavery mail. In fact, from 1835 until the Civil War, there was an unofficial policy agreed to by the Postmasters General of the United States that abolitionist writing was to be kept out of the mail system.[24] Garrison even wrote in *The Liberator* about bias in the press:

> . . . for a quarter of a century abolitionism . . . has been lampooned . . . vilified, unceasingly and universally, by the journals of the day . . . its advocates have been held up as crazy fanatics . . . and its meetings represented as unworthy of countenance by sane and decent men![25]

Prejudice Against African Americans

Printing presses being burned? Mail not being delivered? People being whipped for merely speaking their minds? But Frederick Douglass knew how deep race prejudice went. He wrote about his white abolitionist friends in New England who struggled with their deep-rooted feelings:

> I found this prejudice very strong. . . . When it was said to me, "Mr. Douglass, I will walk to meeting with you; I am not afraid of a black man," I could not help thinking—seeing nothing very frightful in my appearance—"and why should you be?" The children of the north had all been educated to believe that if they were bad, the old *black* man—not the old *devil*—would get them. . . . [26]

A Fight to the Finish

Even though both men disagreed about how to end slavery, they never gave up. After each setback in the law, they counterpunched with an answering opinion. When President Lincoln announced the Emancipation Proclamation in 1863, Douglass wrote, "I never saw enthusiasm before. Men, women, young and old, were up. Hats and bonnets were in the air and we gave three cheers for Abraham Lincoln and three cheers for almost everybody else."[27] Garrison wrote in the final issue of *The Liberator* that it is, "Better to be always in a minority of one . . . branded as a madman . . . fanatic . . . frowned upon by 'the powers that be,' and mobbed by the populace . . . in defense of the right. . . . "[28]

It was not to last. The first Civil Rights legislation passed by Congress in 1875, which declared that all citizens were equal and entitled to all privileges under the law, was judged to be unconstitutional by the Supreme Court of the United States in 1883. It would not be until the 1960s that the law would grant full civil rights to the grandchildren of slaves.

LEGACY OF HATE

ALL THE DIFFERENT STORIES HERE PROVIDE A glimpse into how actual people viewed slavery in America. Depending on their particular experiences, each person confidently believed certain ideas, and misjudged others because of it.

The Slave Trader

John Newton was astonished at his own blindness to the injustice of slavery while he was the captain of a slave trading ship. He never gave a thought that what he was doing might be wrong. In Newton's time, many white people believed that if someone did not worship Jesus, then that person was an ignorant savage. Also, people with dark skin were seen as bad because they represented wickedness in the religion of the Europeans. White people believed they were good because white represented righteousness and purity in their religious faith too. Africans worshipped their own gods and thrived within their own unique cultures, but many white people did not understand these cultures. They did not comprehend that another way of life might be as vital as their own.

The Slaves

Olaudah Equiano was happy living in his village in the Kingdom of Benin. Olaudah never gave a thought that someday he might be kidnapped and taken from his family across the ocean. He had never seen white men before and, at first, believed they would eat him. They put him in a hot and stifling ship's hold with sick and terrified people. Olaudah had no knowledge of the South or the money that was made from the slave trade. He was not used to the utter cruelty that was perpetrated against him and the others on the ship with him. But like Henry Bibb, Equiano felt that it was wrong for one person to own another. The reason why Equiano and Bibb could feel this way is because they perceived whites and blacks as equally human. Many whites did not.

Harriet Jacobs fled from slavery because of the extreme abuse she was forced to endure. Many slaves like her refused the continued torment and ran away. Jacobs not only had the courage to escape and save her family, but also sincerely told her story to others even though it was painful for her.

The Scientific Racist

Scientist and slaveowner Joseph Le Conte wholeheart-edly believed that people who had dark skin were inferior to those with white skin. Le Conte was a supporter of polygenism, a conviction that physical differences in people were directly connected to their intelligence and that these differences made some people inferior. Later, this idea would be considered racism. This "scientific" thinking became the excuse for slavery.

To people like Le Conte, black slaves were too childlike, unskilled, and unintelligent to take care of themselves. Many whites felt that slavery was a wise thing because it taught blacks how to be "civilized." In reality, most whites could not admit openly to themselves that *they* were the dependent ones. The entire Southern civilization had been built on the enslavement of African-American labor.

The Southern Daughter

Letitia Burwell's story of her life as a Southern belle was another side of white dependency on black slave labor. A young girl growing up under paternalism could not see that her society was walking a fine edge between the myth of the happy slave and the unspoken fears of slave revolt. Either slaves loved their masters or they did not. It seems strange that Southern slave owners could believe both things at the same time, but they did. While Southerners loved to glorify the sweetness of slaves contentedly singing in the fields, they also hid their deepest fears of angry slaves wanting to take revenge against their captors. Within their own hearts, many slave owners believed that it was wrong to own another person, just like Henry Bibb and Olaudah Equiano. But they had too much at stake to admit it to themselves. To confess their error meant they would have to renounce generations of Southern tradition. They could not do it.

The Abolitionists

William Lloyd Garrison and Frederick Douglass differed in their approaches, but not in their ultimate goal: to end slavery. Garrison led the charge of the abolitionist movement, while Douglass helped carry it all the way to the Civil War. Even after the war had started, Douglass helped convince President Abraham Lincoln that African Americans should be allowed to fight against the South.

Post-War Violence

After the Civil War forcibly ended slavery, it did not mean that attitudes changed. White Americans held to their mistaken beliefs and fears and devised other means to oppress blacks since owning another human being was now against the law. In 1865, a terrorist organization called the Ku Klux Klan (KKK) was formed. These terrorists had the enthusiastic backing of former slave owners. Its creed demanded "a white man's government in this country," and the group professed to promote "Chivalry, Humanity, Mercy, and Patriotism."[1] Membership in this group became widespread as planters and poor whites joined forces and donned white robes to terrorize African Americans by burning down their homes, stealing from them, and beating and lynching them. The KKK wore white hoods to conceal their faces.

The worst form of terror against black Americans was the practice of lynching. A white mob would gather and pretend that they were administering "justice" by hanging and burning a black person from a nearby tree. They usually accused the black person of a crime, but never gave him or her a fair trial. Most lynchings took place between 1890 and 1920, but it still happens today.[2] In 1999, in Jasper, Texas, African-American James Byrd, Jr. was chained to the back of a truck and dragged to death by three white men. The

Lynchings in the United States peaked at the turn of the twentieth century. However, they still occur today.

Jasper County prosecutor described the murder as a lynching: "Three robed riders came straight out of hell. . . . Instead of a rope, they used a chain, and instead of horses, they had a pick-up truck."[3]

Jim Crow Laws

After slavery, new laws were quickly written. They were called "Jim Crow Laws" and they made sure that black

African-American sharecroppers sometimes had to seek work at the very plantations on which they were once enslaved.

laborers would still be under the thumb of the planters. Many former slaves still worked the same land, but now were farming as sharecroppers. This was a system of labor that continued to exploit black workers. Some of these laws limited where blacks could buy or rent housing. Some laws, called "vagrancy laws," forced blacks to work for plantation owners whether they wanted to or not. Blacks who quit their jobs could be arrested and jailed. Blacks could not testify in court against whites. A black person could be fined for making a speech that whites did not like or for insulting a white person. The worst of the laws took away a black person's right to vote in any election.[4]

Throughout the late nineteenth and most of the twentieth century, local Jim Crow laws were established to keep black Americans from living in the same neighborhoods as whites, from going to the same schools as whites, or from riding in the same railroad cars. Blacks were even banned from drinking out of the same water fountains as whites. This was called segregation.

The Fight Against Segregation

To curb these impulses by prejudiced whites, federal laws were passed during the 1960s that prohibited discrimination against people because of their race.

These laws were called Civil Rights laws. They were enacted after many years of protests by blacks and whites needing federal government help. Like Frederick Douglass, Reverend Martin Luther King Jr., the most famous leader of the Civil Rights Movement, realized that only political methods could affect needed reform. He knew that a person could not wait for the hearts and minds of whites to change. He even wrote

SOURCE DOCUMENT

For more than two centuries our forebears labored in this country without wages; . . . they built the homes of their masters while suffering gross injustice and shameful humiliation—and yet out of a bottomless vitality they continued to thrive and develop. If the inexpressible cruelties of slavery could not stop us, the opposition we now face will surely fail. We will win our freedom because the sacred heritage of our nation and the eternal will of God are embodied in our echoing demands.[5]

In his "Letter From a Birmingham Jail," Martin Luther King, Jr., declares that since African Americans overcame an institution as cruel as slavery, they can surely overcome the injustices of segregation.

in his famous "Letter from a Birmingham Jail:" "Justice delayed is justice denied."

Falsehoods and Unfortunate Facts

White beliefs about living equally with black Americans did not change even with new Civil Rights laws. Whites moved out of neighborhoods when blacks moved in. As late as 1990, a poll taken by the University of Chicago's National Opinion Research Center revealed that 62 percent of non-blacks thought that blacks were lazier than other groups, 56 percent felt they were more prone to violence, 53 percent saw blacks as less intelligent and 78 percent thought they were more likely to be on welfare.[6] These biased viewpoints have persisted since people like Joseph Le Conte promoted them during the days of slavery. They have caused much hardship and inequity for African Americans.

Sad facts today speak for themselves. More young black men end up in prison than enter college. Segregated inner-city public schools do not have enough textbooks for black students because mostly white state governments have financially starved these schools for decades, while suburban white schools enjoy more resources. Racial discrimination still exists in America's job scene as very few companies hire African-American executives and, in 1994, the number of blacks without work was twice that of whites.[7] False

Martin Luther King, Jr., worked to help African Americans reach for true equality.

beliefs of racial inferiority persist and continue to hurt African Americans and other people of color because public policy is primarily based on the views of whites.

All the different views of slavery in this book illustrate the diverse personalities who experienced it. From the theories of the polygenists like Le Conte to the abolitionists like Garrison and Douglass fighting for the end of slavery, people grew up believing certain things that mattered to them. These differing attitudes clashed on many levels until the Civil War finally ended slavery as a *legal* institution.

However, it did not immediately change the hearts and minds of white Americans. The end of slavery, though, did start a long march toward equality that continues today. Committed leaders like Frederick Douglass, Booker T. Washington, W.E.B. DuBois, and Martin Luther King Jr. have created a legacy upon which modern African-American leaders have continued to build. Blacks and whites are talking more about their joint legacy of racism. Teachers are incorporating more ethnic histories into the mosaic of American culture than ever before. There is much to rejoice about, but there is much more work to be done.

✦ T I M E L I N E ✦

1517	Slave trading in the New World begins.
1621	Dutch West Indian Company formed.
1672	English Royal African Company formed.
1750	John Newton gets his own slave trading ship, the *Duke of Argyle*.
1755	Olaudah Equiano is captured in Africa around the age of ten; John Newton quits slave trading.
1766	Olaudah Equiano buys freedom.
1797	Olaudah Equiano dies; William Lloyd Garrison born.
1807	John Newton dies.
1813	Harriet Jacobs is born.
1815	Henry Bibb is born.
1818	Frederick Douglass is born.
1823	Joseph Le Conte is born.
1831	The first issue of *The Liberator* is published by William Lloyd Garrison.
1833	New England Anti-Slavery Society established.
1835	Mob takes over post office and destroys anti-slavery mail.
1839	*Amistad* revolt.
1850	Fugitive Slave Act passed.

1852	*Uncle Tom's Cabin* published.
1854	Henry Bibb dies.
1855	Frederick Douglass writes essay "Three Kinds of Abolitionists."
1861	Civil War begins and Harriet Jacobs publishes *Incidents in the Life of a Slave Girl, Written by Herself.*
1863	Abraham Lincoln announces Emancipation Proclamation.
1865	Civil War ends; Congress passes the Thirteenth Amendment.
1865	Ku Klux Klan formed.
1866	Black Codes passed in the South.
1875	Jim Crow laws enacted in the South; William Lloyd Garrison dies.
1895	Letitia Burwell publishes her book *A Girl's Life in Virginia Before the War* (Birth and death dates for Burwell are unknown); Frederick Douglass dies.
1897	Harriet Jacobs dies.
1901	Joseph Le Conte dies.
1963	Dr. Martin Luther King Jr.'s March on Washington.
1964	Voting Rights Act passed.
1968	Fair Housing Act passed.

CHAPTER NOTES

CHAPTER 1. HENRY BIBB: ESCAPE TO FREEDOM

1. Henry Bibb, *Narrative of the Life and Adventures of Henry Bibb, an American Slave, Written By Himself.* (New York: Published by the Author, 1849), p. 64. Electronic Edition, "Documenting the American South," *University of North Carolina at Chapel Hill Libraries,* <http://docsouth.unc.edu/neh/bibb/bibb.html> (May 20, 2001).

2. Ibid., p. 15.

3. Ibid., pp. 15–16.

4. Eugene D. Genovese, *Roll, Jordan, Roll: The World the Slaves Made,* (New York: Vintage Books, 1976), pp. 650–651.

5. Bibb, p. 33.

6. Genovese, p. 650.

7. Charles Joyner, "The World of Plantation Slaves," *Before Freedom Came: African-American Life in the Antebellum South,* (Charlottesville: University Press of Virginia, 1991), p. 60.

8. Bibb, p. 46.

9. Bibb, p. 25.

10. Genovese, p. 391.

11. Bibb, p. 55.

12. Ibid., p. 56.

13. Ibid., p. 59.

14. Genovese, p. 650.

15. John Hope Franklin and Alfred A. Moss Jr., *From Slavery to Freedom,* (New York: McGraw Hill, 1994), pp. 184–185.

16. Bibb, p. 65.

17. Ibid., pp. 67–68.

18. Ibid., p. 80.
19. Ibid., p. 86.
20. Ibid., p. 87.
21. Ibid., p. 122.
22. Ibid., p. 124.
23. Ibid., p. 128.
24. Ibid., p. 147.
25. Ibid., p. xi.

CHAPTER 2. JOHN NEWTON: SLAVE MERCHANT

1. John Newton, *The Journal of a Slave Trader*, eds. Bernard Martin and Mark Spurrell, (London: Epworth Press, 1962), p. x.

2. John Newton, "Letters on His African Hardships and His Conversion by John Newton," *Christian Heritage Library's Past Words*, n.d., <http://www.gospel.com.net/chi/HERITAGEF/Issuenos/ch1207.shtml> (January 26, 2003).

3. Ibid.

4. Ibid.

5. Herbert S. Klein, *The Atlantic Slave Trade*, (London: Cambridge University Press, 1999), p. 79.

6. Newton, p. 9.

7. Ibid., p. xi.

8. Klein, p. 144.

9. "The Story of Africa," BBC World Service, n.d., <http://www.bbc.co.uk/worldservice/africa/features/storyofafrica/9chapter5.shtml> (January 17, 2003).

10. Thomas Howard, ed. *Black Voyage: Eyewitness Accounts of the Atlantic Slave Trade*, (Boston: Little Brown and Company, 1971), p. 91.

11. Newton, p. 22.

12. Ibid., p. 29.

13. Ibid., p. 18.

14. John Newton, "*From* Thoughts Upon the African Slave Trade," *The Norton Anthology of English Literature: The Restoration and Eighteenth Century: Topics,* © 2003–2004, <http://www.wwnorton.com/nto/18century/topic_2/newton.htm> (February 26, 2004).

15. Joseph Miller, "West Central Africa," *The Atlantic Slave Trade,* 2nd ed., ed. David Northrup, (Boston: Houghton Mifflin Co., 2002), p. 51.

16. Ibid., p. 98.

17. Ibid., p. 99.

CHAPTER 3. OLAUDAH EQUIANO: GOODBYE TO AFRICA

1. Olaudah Equiano, *The Interesting Narrative and Other Writings,* (New York: Penguin Books, 1993), p. 32.

2. Ibid., p. 35.

3. Andrew Froiland, "Ibo," n.d., <http://www.emuseum.mnsu.edu/cultural/oldworld/africa/iboculture.html> (February 22, 2003).

4. Something like the modern banjo.

5. Xylophone.

6. Equiano, p. 34.

7. Froiland.

8. Equiano, p. 32.

9. Madeleine Burnside, *Spirits of Passage,* ed. Rosemarie Robotham (New York: Simon and Schuster, 1997), p. 27.

10. Equiano, p. 40.

11. Ibid., p. 47.

12. Ibid., p. 54.

13. Olaudah Equiano, *The Interesting Narrative of the Life of Olaudah Equiano, or Gustavus Vassa, the African, Written by Himself,* (London: Published by the author, 1789), vol. 1, pp. 247–249. Electronic Edition "Documenting the American South," *University of North Carolina at Chapel Hill Libraries,* <http://docsouth.unc.edu/neh/equiano1/equiano1.html> (February 26, 2004).

14. Equiano, *The Interesting Narrative and Other Writings,* p. 55.

15. Ibid.

16. Burnside, pp. 121–122.

17. Equiano, p. 56.

18. Ibid.

19. Ibid.

20. Ibid., p. 58.

21. Burnside, p. 122.

22. Equiano, p. 59.

23. Ibid., p. 60.

24. Vincent Carretta, "Introduction," *Olaudah Equiano: The Interesting Narrative and Other Writings,* (New York: Penguin Books, 1993), p. ix.

CHAPTER 4. JOSEPH LeCONTE: SCIENCE AND RACISM

1. Joseph Le Conte, *The Autobiography of Joseph Le Conte,* ed. William Dallam Armes (New York: D. Appleton and Co., 1901), p. 9.

2. Ibid.

3. Ibid., pp. 12–13.

4. Ibid., p. 23.

5. "The Idea of Race," n.d., <http://www.washington.edu/burkemuseum/kman/the_idea_of_race.htm> (March 7, 2003).

6. Winthrop D. Jordan, *White Over Black: American Attitudes Toward the Negro 1550–1812,* (Chapel Hill: University of North Carolina Press, 1968), p. 7.

7. Le Conte, p. 13.

8. Jordan, pp. 432–433.

9. Ibid., p. 437.

10. Joseph Le Conte, "The Race Problem in the South," *Man and State: studies in applied sociology; popular lectures and discussions before the Brooklyn ethical association,* (New York: D. Appleton and Co., 1892), p. 367.

11. Fatherly.

12. Philip Morgan, "Three Planters and their Slaves," *Race and Family in the Colonial South,* eds. Winthrop D. Jordan and Sheila L. Skemp (Jackson, Mississippi: University Press of Mississippi, 1987), p. 40.

13. John W. Blassingame, *The Slave Community: Plantation Life in the Antebellum South,* (New York: Oxford University Press, 1979), p. 256.

14. Ibid., p. 161.

15. The way the slaves pronounced "Master."

16. Le Conte, *The Autobiography of Joseph Le Conte,* p. 215.

17. Frederick Douglass, "The Slave's Right to Steal," *Frederick Douglass: The Narrative and Selected Writings,* (New York: McGraw Hill, 1984), p. 136.

18. James C. Scott, *Domination and the Arts of Resistance,* (New Haven: Yale University Press, 1990), pp. 10–11.

19. Le Conte, "The Race Problem in the South," p. 376.

CHAPTER 5. LETITIA BURWELL: PAMPERED BLINDNESS

1. Letitia M. Burwell, "A Girl's Life in Virginia Before the War," Electronic Edition. University of North Carolina at Chapel Hill Libraries. *Documenting the American South.* (1895) Dedication <http://docsouth.unc.edu/burwell/burwell.html> (March 22, 2003).

2. Ibid., pp. 2–3.

3. Elizabeth Fox-Genovese, *Within the Plantation Household: Black and White Women of the Old South,* (Chapel Hill: University of North Carolina Press, 1988), p. 81.

4. Ibid., p. 109.

5. Burwell, p. 4.

6. Fox-Genovese, p. 114.

7. Burwell, p. 6.

8. Fox-Genovese, p. 137.

9. Eugene Genovese, *Roll, Jordan, Roll: The World the Slaves Made,* (New York: Random House, 1974), p. 344.

10. Burwell, pp.128–129.

11. Ibid., pp. 158–159.

12. Ibid., p. 162.

13. Ibid., pp. 163–164.

14. Ibid., p. 44.

CHAPTER 6. HARRIET JACOBS: DESPERATE TO LIVE FREE

1. Harriet A. Jacobs, *Incidents in the Life of a Slave Girl,* (Cambridge: Harvard University Press, 1987), p. 114.

2. Ibid.

3. Edward W. Phifer, "Slavery in Microcosm: Burke County, North Carolina," *Plantation, Town and Country,* eds. Elinor Miller and Eugene D. Genovese (Chicago: University Press of Illinois, 1974), p. 83.

4. Jacobs, p. 6.

5. Ibid., p. 7.
6. Ibid., p. 8.
7. Ibid., p. 9.
8. Ibid., p. 12.
9. Ibid.
10. Ibid., p. 27.
11. Elizabeth Fox-Genovese, *Within the Plantation Household: Black and White Women of the Old South,* (Chapel Hill: University of North Carolina Press, 1988), p. 39.
12. Jacobs, p. 99.
13. Ibid., p. 104.
14. Ibid., p. 105.
15. Ibid., p. 109.
16. Ibid.
17. Ibid., p. 111.
18. Ibid., p. 113.
19. Ibid., p. 115.
20. Ibid., p. 158.
21. Judith S. Levey and Agnes Greenhall, eds., *The Concise Columbia Encyclopedia,* (New York: Columbia University Press, 1983), p. 312.
22. Jacobs, p. 199.
23. Harriet Jacobs, *Incidents in the Life of a Slave Girl,* ed. L. Maria Child (Boston: Published for the author, 1861), p. 114. "Documenting the American South," *University of North Carolina at Chapel Hill Libraries,* 2003, <http://docsouth.unc.edu/jacobs/jacobs.html> (March 1, 2004).

CHAPTER 7. DOUGLASS AND GARRISON: DOWN WITH SLAVERY

1. Frederick Douglass, "Narrative of the Life of Frederick Douglass: An American Slave," *Frederick Douglass: The Narrative and Selected Writings,* (New York: Random House, 1984), p. 11.

2. William Lloyd Garrison, "To the Public," *The Liberator*, January 1, 1831. David W. Blight, "Africans in America," n.d., <http://www.pbs.org/wgbh/aia/part4/4h2928.html> (March 31, 2003).

3. Michael Meyer, "Introduction," *Frederick Douglass: The Narrative and Selected Writings*, (New York: Random House, 1984), pp. 10–11.

4. David W. Blight, "Africans in America," <http://www.pbs.org/wgbh/aia.part4/4p1561.html> (March 31, 2003).

5. Frederick Douglass, *Narrative of the Life of Frederick Douglass, an American Slave. Written by Himself* (Boston: Published At The Anti-Slavery Office, No. 25 Cornhill, 1845), p. 19. Electronic Edition, "Documenting the American South, *University of North Carolina at Chapel Hill Libraries*, 1999, <http://docsouth.unc.edu/douglass/douglass.html> (March 1, 2004).

6. Frederick Douglass, *Life and Times of Frederick Douglass*, (New York: Gramercy Books, 1993), pp. 180–181.

7. Frederick Douglass, "The Liberator and William Garrison," *Frederick Douglass: The Narrative and Selected Writings*, (New York: Random House, 1984), pp. 154–155.

8. Ibid., p. 159.

9. Frederick Douglass, *The Mind and Heart of Frederick Douglass: Excerpts from Speeches of the Great Negro Orator*, ed., Barbara Ritchie (New York: Thomas Y. Crowell Company, 1968), pp. 17–18.

10. Douglass, "The Liberator and William Garrison," p. 160.

11. John Hope Franklin, *From Slavery to Freedom*, (New York: McGraw Hill, 1994), pp. 1973–1974.

12. William E. Cain and Alfred A. Moss Jr., *William Lloyd Garrison and the Fight Against Slavery: Selections from the Liberator*, (Boston: St. Martin's Press, 1995), p. 150.

13. Blight.

14. Richard Rudderman, *Ashbrook Colloqium*, "Frederick Douglass and William Lloyd Garrison," <http://www.ashbrook.org/events/colloqui/2003/ruderman.html> (February 7, 2003).

15. Frederick Douglass, "Various Incidents," *Frederick Douglass: The Narrative and Selected Writings*, (New York: Random House, 1984), p. 166.

16. George M. Fredrickson, ed. *William Lloyd Garrison*, (Englewood, NJ: Prentice-Hall, 1968), p. 92.

17. Frederick Douglass, "Various Incidents," *Frederick Douglass: The Narrative and Selected Writings*, p. 167.

18. Ibid., p. 353.

19. Ibid., p. 355.

20. Ibid., p. 357.

21. Ibid.

22. Ibid., p. 358.

23. Eric Foner, "On the Abolitionist Movement," *Africans in America*, n.d., <http://www.pbs.org/agbh/aia/part4/4i2974.html> (April 1, 2003).

24. William Scarborough, "On the South and the Abolitionist Movement," *Africans in America*, n.d., <http://www.pbs.org/wgbh/aia/part4/4i2979.html> (April 1, 2003).

25. Cain, p. 152.

26. Frederick Douglass, "Abolitionist Lecturer," *Frederick Douglass: The Narrative and Selected Writings*, p. 168.

27. Douglass, *The Mind and Heart of Frederick Douglass*, p. 128.

28. Cain, pp. 182–183.

CHAPTER 8. LEGACY OF HATE

1. William Z. Foster, *The Negro People In American History*, (New York: International Publishers, 1973), p. 327.

2. Danny Postel, "The Awful Truth: Lynching in America," *Znet*, n.d., <http://www.zmag.org/content/showarticle.cfm?SectionID=30&ItemID=2097> (April 14, 2003).

3. Faulknew Fox, "Justice in Jasper," *The Texas Observer*, September 17, 1999, <http://www.texasobserver.org/showArticle.asp?ArticleID=275> (April 15, 2003).

4. John Hope Franklin and Alfred A. Moss Jr., *From Slavery to Freedom*, 7th ed., (New York: McGraw Hill, 1994), p. 225.

5. Martin Luther King, Jr., "Letter From a Birmingham Jail," *University of Pennsylvania—African Studies Center*, n.d., <http://www.sas.upenn.edu/African_Studies/Articles_Gen/Letter_Birmingham.html> (May 12, 2004).

6. Douglas S. Massey and Nancy A. Denton, *American Apartheid*, (Cambridge, Mass.: Harvard University Press, 1993), p. 95.

7. Claudette E. Bennett and Kimberly A. DeBarros, "The Black Population," *U.S. Census Bureau*, n.d., <http://www.census.gov/population/www/pop-profile/blackpop.html> (April 15, 2003).

✦ G L O S S A R Y ✦

ABOLITIONIST—A person who favored ending slavery.

ANTEBELLUM—Latin word meaning "before the war." In this case, the Civil War.

CHATTEL—Property.

COASTING PERIOD—The months spent along the coast of Africa buying slaves to fill the holds of the slave ships.

DISCRIMINATION—Showing intolerance toward people who are different than the majority.

LONGBOATS—The largest boats carried by the slave ships.

MIDDLE PASSAGE—The route where slaves were carried from the coast of Africa to America or the West Indies.

OVERSEER—A white man hired by a planter to manage and punish the slaves on a plantation.

SEGREGATION—Forced separation of racial groups.

SHARECROPPERS—After the Civil War, people who would work a planter's farm in return for a percentage of the crop.

SLAVE TRADER—A captain of a slave ship that transported slaves to America and the West Indies.

UNDERGROUND RAILROAD—A secret set of connections set up by black and white abolitionists to aid slaves escaping from the South.

✧ FURTHER ✦
READING

Carnes, Jim. *Us and Them: A History of Intolerance in America*. New York: Oxford University Press, 1996.

Garrison, Mary. *Slaves Who Dared: The Stories of Ten African-American Heroes*. Shippensburg, Pa.: White Mane Kids, 2002.

Gorrell, Gena K. *North Star to Freedom: The Story of the Underground Railroad*. New York: Delacorte Press, 1997.

Hamilton, Virginia. *Many Thousand Gone: African Americans From Slavery to Freedom*. New York: Knopf, 1993.

Haskins, Jim. *Get on Board: The Story of the Underground Railroad*. New York: Scholastic, 1993.

Hatt, Christine. *Slavery: From Africa to the Americas*. History in Writing Series. New York: Peter Bedrick Books, 1997.

Landau, Elaine, comp. *Slave Narratives: The Journey to Freedom*. New York: Franklin Watts, 2001.

Lester, Julius. *To Be a Slave*. New York: Dial Books, 1998.

———. *Long Journey Home: Stories from Black History*. New York: Dial Books, 1993.

Yetman, Norman, ed. *Voices From Slavery: 100 authentic Slave Narratives*. Mineola, N.Y.: Dover, 2000.

Young, Mary and Gerald Horne, eds. *Testaments of Courage: Selections from Men's Slave Narratives*. New York: Franklin Watts, 1995.

Zeinert, Karen. *The Amistad Slave Revolt and American Abolition*. North Haven, Conn.: Linnet Books, 1997.

INTERNET ← ADDRESSES

THE AFRICAN-AMERICAN MOSAIC
LIBRARY OF CONGRESS RESOURCE GUIDE TO BLACK
HISTORY AND CULTURE
http://www.loc.gov/exhibits/african/intro.html

AFRICANS IN AMERICA
PUBLIC BROADCASTING CORPORATION
http://www.pbs.org/wgbh/aia/home.html

AMERICAN SLAVE NARRATIVES: AN ONLINE
ANTHOLOGY
http://xroads.virginia.edu/~HYPER/wpa/wpahome.html

HISTORIC ← SITES

FREDERICK DOUGLASS NATIONAL HISTORIC SITE
1411 W. Street, SE
Washington, DC 20020-4813
202-426-5961

MUSEUM OF AFRO-AMERICAN HISTORY
14 Beacon Street, Suite 719
Boston, MA 02108
617-725-0022
history@afroammuseum.org

INDEX

A

abolitionists, 14, 20, 54, 79–80, 86, 88, 91, 93–97, 102, 110
Africa, 21, 22, 24, 32
Aunt Fanny, 65, 66

B

Benin, 31–32, 100
Bibb, Henry, 7–19
Bibb, Malinda, 10–11, 13, 15, 16, 18
Bibb, Mary Frances, 10–11, 13, 16, 18
"Big House," 60, 67
"bloody flux," 29
Burwell, Letitia, 56, 57–58, 60–62, 64–67

C

Canada, 9, 13
Christianity, 99
civil rights, 98, 106–107
Civil War, the, 20, 52, 57, 67, 84, 93, 96, 103, 110
"coasting period," 24
Constitution, 90
  as anti–slavery document, 91, 93, 94

D

Daddy Dick, 44, 45
discrimination, 106, 108
Douglass, Frederick, 54, 82, 83–86, 88, 90, 91, 93–95, 97, 107
"down river," 13
Dutch West India Company, 23

E

Emancipation Proclamation, 97
English Royal African Company, 23
Equiano, Olaudah, 30, 31–32, 34–39, 41–43

F

Flint, Dr., 68, 71–72, 74–75, 79
Free Soil Party, 93
Fugitive Slave Act, 79, 91

G

Garrison abolitionists, 93, 94
Garrison, William Lloyd, 82, 83–84, 86, 88, 90–91, 93, 94, 95, 96, 97–98

"Great Chain of Being, The," 47

I
Ibo, 31, 32, 42, 100

J
Jacobs, Harriet, 67, 68–72, 74–75, 77–82, 100–101
Jefferson, Thomas, 48–49
Jim Crow laws, 105–106
"jumping the broom," 10

K
King, Martin Luther, Jr., 107–108, 110
Ku Klux Klan (KKK), 103

L
Le Conte, Joseph, 44–49, 51–52, 54–56, 101
Liberator, The, 82, 84, 86, 88, 96, 97–98
Louisiana, 13, 16
Lovejoy, Elijah, 95–96
lynching, 103, 105

M
Middle Passage, 24–25, 28, 30, 39, 41

N
Newton, John, 21–30
New England Anti–Slavery Society, 88–89
New York, 74

Norcom, James. *See* Flint, Dr.
North Star, The, 93

P
paternalism, 49, 51, 56, 60, 67, 72, 101–102
Philadelphia, Pa., 78, 82
plantations
  Burwell, 57, 58
  Gatewood, 10,13
  Otterburn, 64
  Woodmanston, 44, 46
polygenism, 47–49, 55–56, 101, 110

Q
Quakers, 23, 79, 80

R
racism, 101, 108, 110
radical abolitionists, 93, 94–95
Republican Party, 93–94

S
segregation, 106–107
sharecroppers, 106
Sherman, William T., 52
slavery,
  in Africa, 32, 34
  in the British colonies, 19
  chattel, 18, 41–42, 69, 70–71, 75, 79–80, 83

conditions aboard slave ships, 26–29, 37–39, 41

escape, 9, 68–69, 75, 77–79, 86

happiness of slaves, 46–47, 51–52, 58, 85

legacy of, 20, 99–103, 105–108, 110

mistreatment of slaves, 11, 18, 37, 39, 41, 45, 51–52, 60–62, 71–72, 74, 88

religious beliefs of slaves, 24, 31, 66, 100

resistance to, 54–55, 64–65, 72, 84

slave holders, 12, 13, 49, 51, 56, 57–58, 81, 85, 102

slave hunters, 9, 14

slave traders, 21, 34–37, 74–75, 99

white blindness to cruelty of, 30, 58, 83

southern culture, 58, 60

religion,70–71, 81

resistance to abolitionists, 95

slave/mistress relationship, 64, 70–71

white slaveholding women, 61–62, 66–67

T

Thirteenth Amendment, 19, 112

Triangular Trade, 19, 24–25

U

Underground Railroad, 14, 93

V

vagrancy laws, 106

voting, 55–56, 91, 93

Voting Rights Act of 1964, 56

W

Wheatley, Phillis, 49